**ANTHROPOLOGICAL PAPERS**

MUSEUM OF ANTHROPOLOGY, UNIVERSITY OF MICHIGAN
NO. 27



# THE PALEO-INDIAN OCCUPATION OF THE HOLCOMBE BEACH

BY
JAMES E. FITTING
JERRY DEVISSCHER
EDWARD J. WAHLA

ANN ARBOR
THE UNIVERSITY OF MICHIGAN, 1966

ISBN (print): 978-1-949098-18-1
ISBN (ebook): 978-1-951519-41-4

Browse all of our books at
sites.lsa.umich.edu/archaeology-books.

Order our books from the University of Michigan
Press at www.press.umich.edu.

For permissions, questions, or manuscript queries,
contact Museum publications by email at umma-pubs@umich.edu or visit the Museum website at
lsa.umich.edu/ummaa.

## PREFACE

The Holcombe site is one of the sites excavated by the University of Michigan Museum of Anthropology between 1960 and 1962. These excavations were conducted with the support of a National Science Foundation grant (65-86) entitled "A Correlation of Prehistoric Cultural Complexes and Post Glacial Ecologies in the Upper Great Lakes" and were under the direction of James B. Griffin. This monograph is one of a series of reports on the project which will eventually cover the period from the first retreat of glacial ice in Michigan to the coming of the Europeans.

The site was discovered by Mr. Jerry DeVisscher of Mount Clemens, Michigan. He assisted the University of Michigan Museum of Anthropology field party in 1961 and continued excavations in the area of the site after we left. Working by himself and with Mr. Edward J. Wahla and other members of the Aboriginal Research Club of Detroit, DeVisscher found three additional Paleo-Indian sites within a short distance of the Holcombe site. DeVisscher and Wahla prepared reports on these sites which are included in the present study, and in addition to their contribution of three papers, have read and commented on other parts of this volume. Throughout the past five years, I have learned much from these men and should like to thank them not only for their aid in preparing this report, but for the insight which they have given to me on the prehistory of southeastern Michigan in general.

I have also benefited from association with Arthur J. Jelinek of the University of Michigan Museum of Anthropology. Jelinek's knowledge of flint knapping and his notes from the 1964 Les Eyzies Conference on lithic technology have proved invaluable. He has read all of Parts I and III and has made valuable comments on earlier versions of these sections. James B. Griffin has also read and commented on these sections and his assistance is gratefully acknowledged.

In preparing the first part of this study, Mrs. Anta M. White made many helpful comments and suggestions. Richard I. Ford was equally as helpful in preparing the final section. Other persons who read and commented upon earlier versions of parts of this study were Douglas S. Byers, Don E. Crabtree, and William B. Roosa. William R. Farrand, of the University of Michigan Geology Department, and William S. Benninghoff, of the Botany Department, were of great assistance in preparing those sections which deal with their respective areas of study.

The maps were drawn by George Stuber of the University of Michigan Museum of Anthropology. The drawings in Figures 4 through 9 were made by myself with the exception of Figure 5, *b* and *d* and Figure 6, *e* and *f* which were done by Jane Pollock while taking a course in Museum Techniques in the fall of 1964. The drawings in Figures 16 through 20 are by Edward J. Wahla although I retraced and rearranged them for this publication. I must take the responsibility for the loss of some detail from Wahla's originals. I have attempted to match each drawing with a photograph. The photographs in Plates II through XII were taken by George Stuber and mounted by myself; those in Plate I were taken by Richard O. Keslin at the time the site was excavated. While more than 220 artifacts are illustrated they represent less than one-third of those recovered from the sites. Many of these artifacts, however, are extremely small and fragmentary while almost all of the major artifacts and artifact variants are included in the present illustrations.

Quotations from *People of the Deer* are reprinted with permission of Little, Brown and Company.

Earlier drafts of this report were typed by Wahla and myself. Miss Frances Steketee, Miss Yolanda Gable, Mrs. Ruth Hull and the University of Michigan office services typed subsequent drafts. My wife, Molly, deserves special commendation for proofreading many drafts of this report. Final editing was done by Mrs. Clara Johnston of the University Publications Office.

Once again, I should like to acknowledge the support of the National Science Foundation which helped to make this study possible.

James E. Fitting

## CONTENTS

### PART I: THE HOLCOMBE SITE

*James E. Fitting*



### PART II: OTHER PALEO-INDIAN SITES ALONG THE HOLCOMBE BEACH

*Jerry DeVisscher and Edward J. Wahla*



### PART III: THE PALEO-INDIAN OCCUPATION OF THE HOLCOMBE BEACH

*James E. Fitting*

## PLATES

(Plates I-XII follow page 147)

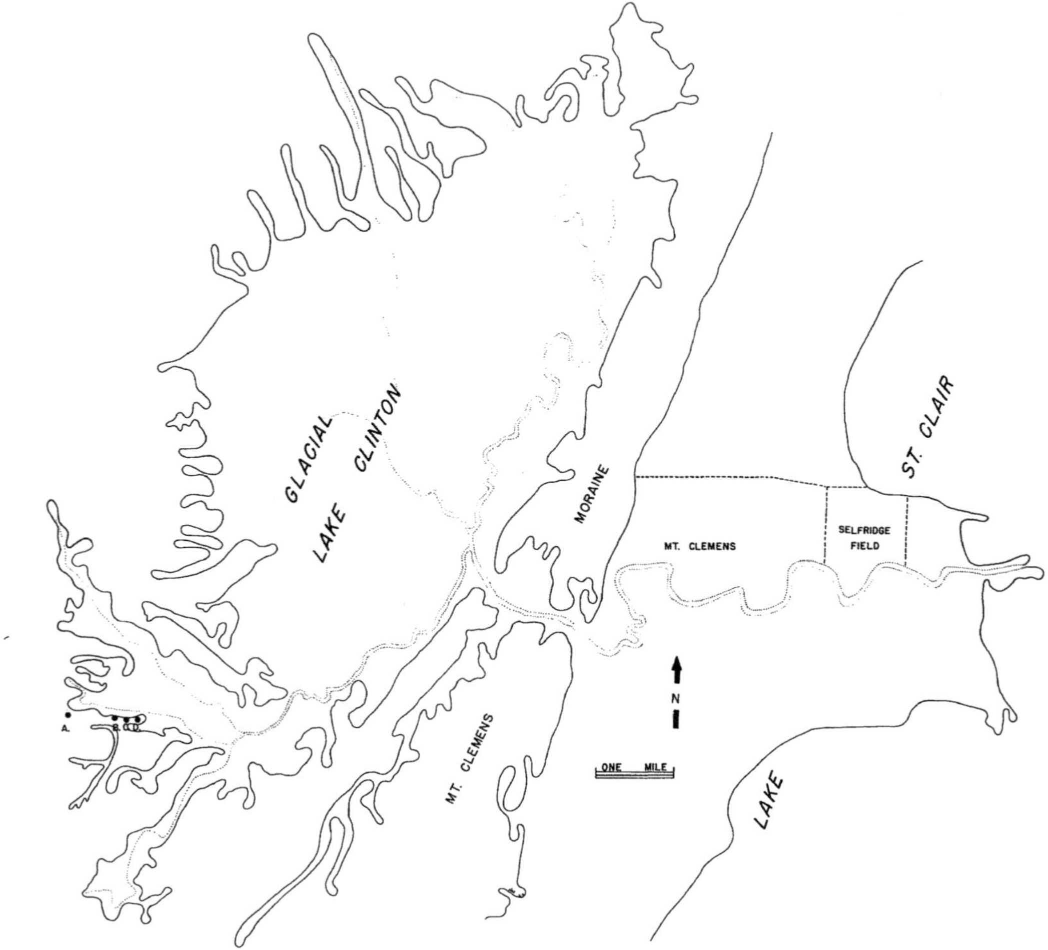


FIG. 1. Map showing the location of glacial Lake Clinton in relation to modern features. (A) The Holcombe site, (B) Paleo-II-W,(C.) Paleo-II-W-A,(D.) Paleo-II.

# PART I

# THE HOLCOMBE SITE

James E. Fitting

## I

## THE SITE

### Description and Geological History

The Holcombe site is located in the southwest quarter of the southwest quarter of section 23 of Sterling Township, Macomb County, Michigan. The site is within view of both Dodge Road and 16 Mile Road. It is located on a sand ridge with an elevation slightly over 605 feet above sea level. The sand ridge runs parallel to, and about 300 yards north of, 16 Mile Road. About 300 yards to the east of Dodge Road the sand ridge turns to the south where it crosses 16 Mile Road close to the junction with Dodge Road.

When we first visited the site it was a rural area with a strong urban orientation. This part of Macomb County had been known as a rhubarb-growing area but many of the farms were sod farms in 1962. Everywhere the sod farmer and the sand broker were altering the landscape. One mile to the west along Van Dyke Road the inevitable subdivisions were being built. At the present moment the Holcombe sod farm is still intact, but three nearby Paleo-Indian sites, Paleo-II, Paleo-II-W, and Paleo-II-W-A, have been destroyed by roads and buildings. Within the next few years the last of this unique series of sites will be engulfed by the expanding city.

The Holcombe site lies on a sand ridge which had been formed in the distant past. Its history is interwoven with the late glacial history of the Great Lakes and southeastern Michigan. We shall review this history by means of one of the most recent of the geological summaries of the Great Lakes prepared by Jack

Hough (1963). This summary contains some revisions of his earlier work (1958) and requires a certain amount of reinterpretation of earlier studies of Paleo-Indian remains in the Great Lakes area.

The bedrock formation underlying the site is a soft Devonian shale. This is deeply buried beneath later glacial till. It has been suggested that in preglacial times the areas under the present-day lakes were broad river valleys eroded into the softer rock. Almost all traces of these earlier valleys were destroyed by later ice movement.

According to Hough, the first of the Great Lakes was formed 15,000 years ago. Throughout the first third of the lakes existence, the Holcombe site was either covered by glacial ice or glacial lakes. Occupation would have been possible during the Cary-Port Huron interval, but any sites representing such an occupation would have been flooded and disturbed by high-water stages created by the Port Huron ice advance.

The site as it stands today would have become habitable during an early stage of glacial Lake Algonquin which had an elevation of 605 feet above sea level. In early post-Port Huron times the higher-level lakes drained to the north by way of a strait which followed the present St. Clair channel, through the Lake Michigan basin, and down the Chicago outlet. Sometime during this period the eastern ice front retreated sufficiently to allow water from the Lake Huron basin to flow southward through the St. Clair channel, through Lake Erie, and over Niagara Falls, as it does today.

During the brief low-water stage between early and main Lake Algonquin, the area which is now Lake St. Clair was dry. Hough has correlated this low stage with the Two Creeks interval which, on the basis of radiocarbon dating (Broecker and Farrand, 1963), ended about 11,800 years ago. With the full Valders advance around 11,500 years ago the water level in the Michigan and Huron basins again rose to 605 feet above sea level (main Algonquin stage). Griffin (1965) has discussed the archaeological implications of the sequence in some detail.

The main Algonquin stage occurred during, and immediately following, the maximum of the Valders ice advance. Then, as the Valders ice retreated farther, there was a very rapid drop in lake levels producing a series of post-Lake Algonquin beaches, the lowest of which, the Chippewa Stanley low stage, was reached by at least 9,500 years ago and perhaps earlier. At this time the Holcombe site would have been located on a high and dry plateau.

Hough then postulated a gradual rise in lake level in the upper lakes over the next 5,000 years culminating in the Nipissing lake stage, the last of the high lake levels with an elevation of 605 feet above sea level. This level was reached slightly over 4,000 years ago. Following this high stage Lake Huron dropped to its present elevation, probably sometime around 3,000 years ago. Based on suggestions from the distribution of archaeological sites there appears to have been little change in the last 2,500 years.

The Holcombe site itself is not directly located on Lake St. Clair. It is behind the Mount Clemens moraine (Bay, 1938: 54-5) and the Lake Algonquin beach in this area parallels Gratiot Avenue on the east of the moraine. James W. Bay, in his study of streams in southeastern Michigan, noted that there was an area to the west of the Mount Clemens moraine which was under 605 feet in elevation. Since the Clinton River ran through the moraine at the site of the present city of Mount Clemens this area would have been a shallow lake during Lake Algonquin times. Bay called it Lake Clinton. In 1958 Hough suggested that early Lake Algonquin existed in both the Erie and Huron basins and that it drained northward through the area of the St. Clair channel. This stage must have been brief since the early Algonquin beaches are so vague that they have not yet been identified in the Erie basin. With the retreat of the ice which blocked the eastern outlet of the Lake Erie Basin at Niagara Falls the direction of water flow in the area of the St. Clair basin must have been reversed from a northward (postulated by Hough) to a southward flow because the level of Lake Erie was abruptly lowered, while the level in the Lake Huron basin, north of Port Huron, remained at 605 feet above sea level. Therefore, early Lake Algonquin was terminated earlier in the Lake Erie basin than in the Lake Huron Basin.

But what happened during this time in the St. Clair Basin? Hough (1958: 155-59) thought that the moraine south of Port Huron along the present St. Clair channel would have held the main Algonquin level in the Huron basin at 605 feet above sea level while the channel in the area of the Detroit River was at its present level. If this has been the case the level of Lake St. Clair would not have risen over 580 feet in the last 12,000 years.

Leverett and Taylor (1915) and Bay (1938) felt that during periods of southward flow through this channel, as during the main Algonquin stage, the principal obstructions were along the Detroit River with an intermediate lake near the present mouth of the Rouge River, then called Lake Rouge. "Two ridges running roughly northwest-southeast obstructed the flow of water between Lake St. Clair and Lake Erie when these two lakes were first formed. One was the Detroit Interlobate Moraine at the present head of the Detroit River. The second, crossing the river at the present mouth, was a broad flat-topped ridge of ordinary till underlain by a deposit of boulders set in hard till with a core of massive limestone. Between the two ridges a small lake basin existed at the mouth of the Rouge" (Bay, 1938: 52, 54; see Figure 11 for map of this relationship).

We noted the presence of a strong beach at approximately 605 feet above sea level along the Mount Clemens Moraine. Today, Gratiot Avenue roughly follows this ridge. Since the traces of early Lake Algonquin are vague in the Erie basin it should be the same in the St. Clair basin if the drainage barrier had been across only the St. Clair River. The obstruction along the Detroit River suggested by Bay seems to fit the geological evidence better. We would suggest, therefore, that early Lake Algonquin had a similar duration in the Huron and St. Clair basins, whereas that lake stage terminated somewhat earlier in the Lake Erie basin.

There is a lower beach ridge in the present area of Sugarbush Road west of Lake St. Clair. Cultural materials generally held to be in the neighborhood of 6,000 to 10,000 years old (Quimby, 1960: 34-42; Fitting, 1963 *b*; Peske, 1963) are found in an apparently undisturbed condition at elevations below 605 and above 595 feet above sea level in the Lake St. Clair basin (DeVisscher and Wahla, Part II). Such undisturbed artifacts would not be found if the Nipissing stage had existed in the Lake St. Clair basin at a level of 605 feet above sea level. It is possible that the Port Huron moraine held the Nipissing lake level in the Huron basin at 605 feet above sea level while enough erosion had taken place in the Detroit River to allow a more gradual drainage from Lake St. Clair to Lake Erie. The Sugarbush Road beach would have been formed at this time at an elevation of approximately 595 feet above sea level. Sometime after 6,000 B.P. the Detroit River sill was eroded to its present level.

When we traced the 605-foot contour interval on a map for the area now drained by the Clinton River behind the Mount Clemens moraine (Figure 1), we found that the Holcombe site was at the base of a small promontory in Lake Clinton. This promontory is the sand ridge mentioned earlier and is strongly suggestive of a spit formation. Several other sites of the same cultural complex as the Holcombe site were discovered along this ridge. In 1962 this area was too disturbed by sand removal and buildings to trace its maximum extent and shape.

Today, this part of Michigan is in the southern deciduous forest area, and is a part of Dice's (1943) Carolinian Biotic Province. In the early contact period it was sparsely settled, perhaps caused by its border position between warring groups of Iroquois and Algonquin. Excluding hearsay accounts we cannot speak of the Indian inhabitants of this part of Michigan until 1701 when Detroit was founded. At that time a number of Indian tribes entered the area to trade with the French. The site is very close to the place where the Moravian Mission Indians established their settlement in the late eighteenth century.

Evidence for historic use of the land was presented in the course of excavation by discovery of buttons, thimbles, coins, and horseshoe nails in the plow zone. Those objects which could be dated suggested a considerable time span starting with an 1854 Indian head penny, running through 1864 with a dated Chillcoth meat market token, to the twentieth century. The farm which stands on the site is a Centennial Farm so we have ample evidence that cultivation had been carried on for well over a century before we arrived at the site.

## Discovery and Earlier Reports

The site was located in 1960 by Jerry DeVisscher of Mount Clemens, Michigan. DeVisscher has done extensive collecting in Macomb County and adjacent areas and is, himself, a flint knapper of some note. He recognized the importance of the site and contacted Professor Arnold R. Pilling of Wayne State University. Pilling visited the site with DeVisscher and several students in the spring of 1961. At that time the Wayne State University Museum of Anthropology was unable to field a permanent crew for the period of time which would be required to excavate the site. (It was possible for the University of Michigan Museum of Anthropology to field such a crew so Pilling suggested that we undertake the actual excavation of the site. The extent of these excavations were described in Chapter II.

Some confusion arose on site numbering. DeVisscher had used the designation of D 36 in his records and also used this number in cataloging all of the artifacts in his collection from the site. The Wayne State University Museum of Anthroplogy recorded the site as 20 MB 150. There are no records as to how it happened, but in the spring of 1961 someone at The University of Michigan recorded the site as 20 MB 30 although there was already a site for this number. The error in numbering was discovered after the material had been cataloged so arrangements were made to switch the site number. 20 MB 30 is now the Holcombe site number in the files of both Universities.

A number of reports of certain aspects of the site have appeared, and several papers dealing with limited parts of the collection from the site have been presented at professional meetings. There are a number of references to material from the site in *Chips from the Totem Pole*, published by Edward J. Wahla in 1961 and 1962.

A summary paper dealing with a part of the collection from the site was presented by Richard O. Keslin at the Society for American Archaeology and Central States Anthropological Society meetings in 1963 and at the meeting of the Michigan Academy of Science, Arts, and Letters in 1964.

I made a quantitative examination of some of the basal fragments in 1962. In 1963 I prepared a paper on this analysis as a part of a directed study project taken under Arthur J. Jelinek. This paper was presented at the 1963 meeting of the Michigan Academy of Science, Arts, and Letters and was published in the *Papers* for that year, which appeared in 1964.

Charles E. Cleland, who participated in the excavation and served as paleo-zoologist for the Museum of Anthropology until he joined the staff of Michigan State University, identified some of the bone fragments from the site as barren-ground Caribou. The results of his work and the basis for his identification appeared in the Facts and Comments section of *American Antiquity* in 1965.

Plant material from the site was studied in 1961 and 1962 by Richard Yarnell, then of the University of Michigan Museum of Anthropology. Yarnell included this data in his doctoral dissertation, which was accepted in 1963. In 1964 this analysis was published as a part of *Anthropological Paper No. 23* of the University of Michigan Museum of Anthropology.

In 1962 DeVisscher found a second Paleo-Indian site to the east of the Holcombe site. This was called Paleo-II and was reported by DeVisscher and Wahla in *The Totem Pole* in 1963. In 1963 DeVisscher found a third Paleo-Indian site on the same sand spit which he called Paleo-II-W. A report on this site was written by DeVisscher and Wahla and published in both *The Totem Pole* and *The Michigan Archaeologist*. True to form, DeVisscher discovered a fourth site on the same sand spit in 1964 which he called Paleo-II-W-A. The results of this report are included in this paper along with revised versions of the two earlier reports by DeVisscher and Wahla.

Although the Holcombe site was the first of the series of sites to be excavated, the fact that the other two sites were reported at an earlier time influenced the present report. As an example, I have not given a detailed description of the techniques used in fluting or altering the bases of the projectile points from the site since Wahla and DeVisscher had already done so. I was aware of differences and similarities between these sites when writing the report on the Holcombe site itself. These differences and similarities will be discussed in Part III of this paper; but in the meantime it is important for the reader to realize that they exist. With this survey of previous publications we shall present the analysis of cultural material from the Holcombe site.

# II

## UNIVERSITY OF MICHIGAN EXCAVATIONS AT THE HOLCOMBE SITE

### Nature and Extent of Excavation

University of Michigan excavations at the Holcombe site were undertaken during two periods. On April 8, 1961, Mark Papworth opened two test pits on the site with a crew consisting of Robert Bettarel, Bill and Nancy Buckles, Charles Cleland, Christy Cogan, and David Taggart. These two 10- by 10-foot units were designated as 120-100 and 140-100. These designations were tied into a stake by the fence line separating the main area of the site from a field to the south between the site and 16 Mile Road. Between this time and our return to the site two months later, the fence posts were taken out and the fence line plowed so we were not able to locate these units.

The April test excavations were very productive. In one day several bases and retouched flakes, along with several small retouch flakes, were recovered. It was decided that a full season of excavation would be profitable and a crew returned to the site in June.

Between June 19, 1961, and July 28, 1961, a crew consisting of Charles Cleland, James E. Fitting, Larry Robbins, and David Taggart worked at the site under the direction of Richard O. Keslin. During this time we excavated twenty-three 10- by 10-foot units, three 5- by 10-foot units, and one 5- by 5-foot unit which gave us a total excavated area of 2,675 square feet on the site (Figure 2).

Our excavation units clustered in three areas which were determined primarily by concentrations of surface material. We opened several additional units in outlying areas to test the stratigraphy and distribution of cultural materials. We also extended our excavations to include rather large areas around these surface concentrations. In all instances the amount of subsurface cultural material appeared to be directly correlated with the amount of surface material.

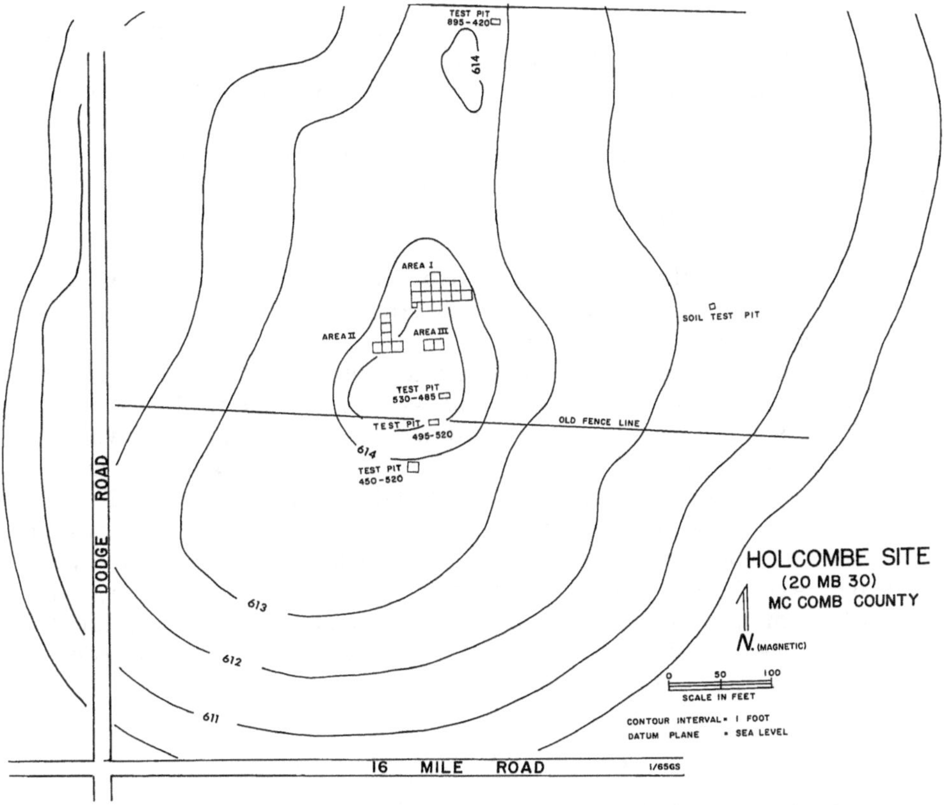


FIG. 2. Map of the Holcombe site showing areas excavated by the University of Michigan Museum of Anthropology.

The largest cluster of excavation units centered around unit 620-500 which contained three of the eight features at the site (Figure 3). This cluster will be designated as Area I in the analysis of the site. It consisted of fourteen 10 by 10-foot units and one 5- by 5- foot unit which was opened to trace a possible feature.

The second cluster, a group of six 10- by 10-foot units, was excavated to the southwest of Area I, hereinafter cited as Area II. It too, represents the "working out" of a surface concentration.

There was no great concentration of surface material in the area of the third group of excavation units. This group of two 10- by 10-foot units, designated as Area III, was opened because of its supposed proximity to 120-100 and 140-100 of the preseason testing. We hoped to locate traces of these two earlier 10- by 10-foot units but were unsuccessful. The material from the April excavations, however, will be included with that from the other two units in our analysis since it represents part of our sample from the southeastern corner of the site.

A single 10- by 10-foot excavation unit was opened in the field to the south of the site. This was unit 450-520 in our grid system for the site. This excavation proved to be so unproductive that we abandoned the area to concentrate our efforts on the richer localities to the north.

A 5- by 10-foot unit was opened along the former fence line. This was unit 530-485 in our grid system. Post molds from the former fence line were uncovered but cultural material was sparse. An additional 5- by 10-foot unit, unit 495-500, was opened in the south field between 450-520 and the fence line.

The last single excavation unit was located on the northern boundary of the field in which the site was located. This was unit 895-420 in the site grid system. It was an interesting unit in that it overlapped an old farm road bordered by parallel rows of maple trees. We excavated several wagon tracks and recovered only historic materials.

## Techniques of Excavation

The techniques used in excavation were standard. Our basic tools were trowels and long-handled, flat-nosed shovels. All of the excavated material was screened through a quarter-inch mesh hardware cloth. At regular intervals samples were run through a fine screen. A number of soil samples were saved. Almost all of the material from features was fine screened.

Shovels would be used until we reached the base of the plow zone. The dark brown sandy loam of the plow zone contrasted with the unplowed yellow sand so we were able to trowel out the plow scars and separate the material from the obviously disturbed and possibly undisturbed areas. Below the plow zone quarter sections of each 10- by 10-foot unit were taken out with separate provenience. The standard level was .3 feet but this varied when features or other obvious disturbances were encountered. By shovel skimming we were able to pick up most of the point bases and other artifacts. These were given specific provenience designation. When such material was recovered in the screen we were able to locate its original position within a 5- by 5-foot by

.3-foot area on the site. Trowels, probes, and brushes were used on features.

The standard University of Michigan Museum of Anthropology square sheets and feature forms were used in the course of excavation. Keslin kept a brief log and an extensive photographic record. Almost every floor and profile on the site was photographically recorded in color, black and white, or both.

## Stratigraphy of the Site

For a sand ridge the subsurface appearance of the Holcombe site was colorful enough. This area was heavily wooded in the preceding century and had been burned off for agricultural purposes. Almost every unit on the site contained charcoal fragments and ash pockets from this burning. Several large burned-out stumps were encountered and several of these were designated and excavated as separate features until we became familiar with their patterns.

Even with the many disturbances it was possible to work out a stratigraphical sequence for the site. In doing this we were assisted by Thomas Gough and Robert Bryan of the Soil Conservation Service in Mount Clemens. The following description is based on tests which were made in unit 590-540, and which was taken down to the water table, but are typical of the entire central area of the site. Five zones, Ap, $A_2$, C, $D_1$, and $D_2$, were recognized by Gough and Bryan. The descriptions, depths, pH and Munsell colors are given below:

*Zone*

Ap. (Plow Zone). Zone Ap is a layer of loamy sand which averages about .65 feet in thickness. The variation in thickness is caused by irregularities on the surface and variation in the depth of plow scars. There is an abrupt boundary between this zone and the $A_2$ zone. The pH is 5.3, slightly acid. This color is dark brown to brown or Munsell color 10 YR 4/3.

$A_2$. Zone $A_2$ is found between the base of the Ap zone (.65 feet below the surface) and 2.0 feet below the surface. The boundary between this zone and the lower C zone is diffuse and irregular. No cultural material was found below this uniform sand level. The pH varied but there were several consistent tests of 4.5 and 4.8. The color of this fine-to-medium sand is yellow to brownish yellow or Munsell color 10 YR 7/6 and 6/6.

C. Level C consists of medium-to-coarse mottled sand and falls between 2.0 and 3.7 feet below the surface. The soil is only slightly acid with a pH of 6.5. Some of the mottling may be caused by water percolation. The boundary between this zone and the $D_1$ zone is distinct, but wavy. The mottling varies between pale red and dark brown with the following percentages of several Munsell colors:

| Series | Color | Percentage | Name |
|---|---|---|---|
| 10 YR. | 6/2 | *Ca.* 10 | Pale red |
| 10 YR | 6/4 | *Ca.* 30 | Pale red |
| 10 YR. | 5/6 | *Ca.* 40 | Red |
| 10 YR. | 5/8 | *Ca.* 15 | Red |
| 7.5 YR. | 4/4 | *Ca.* 5 | Dark brown |

$D_1$. Zone $D_1$ is a coarse sand found between 3.7 and 5.9 feet below the surface. The water table was approximately 4.0 feet below the surface in this unit so coring tools were used to determine the maximum depth. This zone had a pH of 4.5. It had a Munsell color of 10 YR 5/4.

$D_2$. $D_2$ was a clay loam which was found below the water table at a depth of 5.9 feet below the surface. It was a mottled dark greyish brown, Munsell color 10 YR 4/2, to strong brown, Munsell color 7.5 YR 5/6.

The interpretation of the soil profile, a loamy sand surface with sand predominating through the profile, all overlying basal clays, indicates that this was probably a beach formation. This interpretation fits in well with the over-all geological interpretations of the area described in the preceding section.

The soil type is moderately well drained as shown by the mottling in the C horizon. This would indicate that it was generally dry throughout the year. Gough and Bryan suggested that oak and hickory would be the natural vegetation. The area was climax forest a century ago but it seems doubtful if this was the case at the time of the Paleo-Indian occupation.

## Features

During the course of our excavations eight disturbances were designated as feature. Several of these were definitely cultural disturbances while others were without doubt burned out stumps or other natural disturbances. Once we learned to recognize the stumps we no longer gave them feature numbers. The numbers, locations, and descriptions of the features are given below.

### Feature Number 1

Feature Number 1 was located in Area I in the southwest

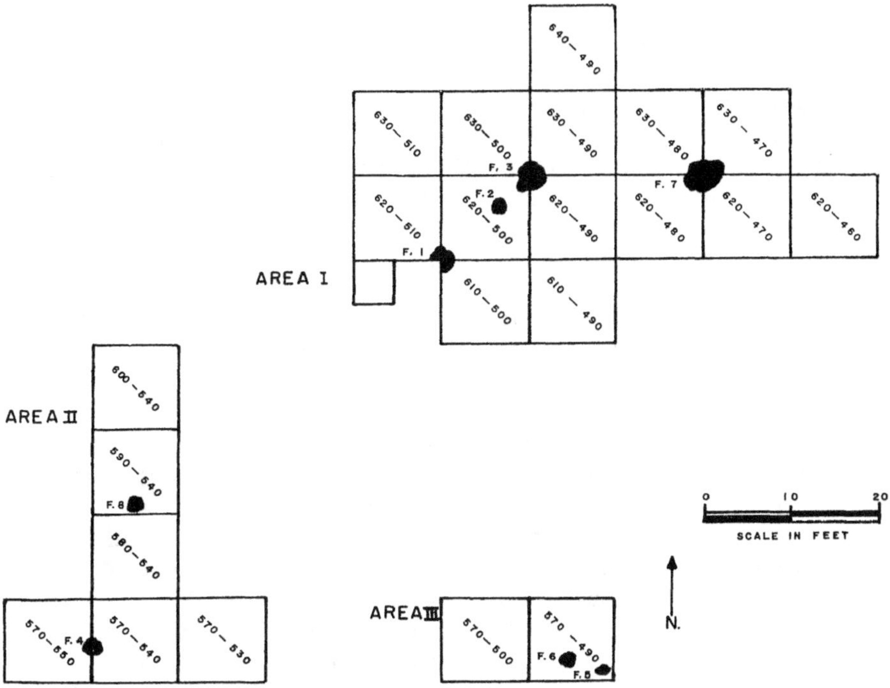


FIG. 3. Location of features in the main area of the Holcombe site.

quarter of unit 620-500 and parts of the adjacent northwest quarter of unit 610-500 (Figure 3) and southeast quarter of 620-510. It was a shallow, basin-shaped depression filled with hard brownish-red sand which was bordered by an area of orange sand darker than the basic yellow sands of the $A_2$ zone. Its maximum north-south measurement was slightly over two feet and its maximum east-west measurement was slightly under two feet. It extended to a depth of .3 feet below the plow zone. Three dark streaks extended to the north and west of this feature for short distances. These streaks are interpreted as rodent burrows, partly filled by the darker contents of the feature. They tended to slope downward. This feature contained very few flint chips and very little charcoal.

## Feature Number 2

Feature Number 2 was first noted as a concentration of bone fragments in a hard brownish matrix in Area I in the southwest quarter of the northeast quarter of unit 620-500. At first it was thought to be connected with Feature Number 3 but further excavation demonstrated that this connection was superficial. This, too, appeared to be a basin-shaped pit filled with hardened brownish sand. It had maximum north-south and east-west measurements of about 1.8 feet and ran to a depth of about .3 feet below the base of the plow zone. Large numbers of bone fragments and flint chips were recovered from this feature. Like Feature Number 1, very little charcoal was recovered. The bone fragments included the remains of a barren-ground caribou which Cleland had discussed at some length (Cleland, 1965).

Feature Number 3

Feature Number 3 was located in the northeast quarter of the northeast quarter of unit 620-500 and the adjacent northwest quarter of the northwest quarter of unit 620-490. It was an irregular area of hard brownish-red sand of varying depths. At its maximum extent it had an 8 foot east-west measurement and a 6 foot north-south measurement. At its deepest point it ran to 1.6 feet below the surface or .9 feet below the plow zone. In the very center, at the base of the plow scars, there was a concentration of charcoal and ash. Obvious root patterns and occasional pockets of decayed organic material were noted. The interpretation given to this feature while in the field was that it was a decomposed tree stump. This was further borne out by the relative sparsity of cultural material in this area. It is possible that part of the root pattern of this tree overlay Feature Number 2 and that the burning of this stump caused the apparent connection between these features in the level just below the plow zone. Yarnell (1964:197) identified the charcoal from this feature as beech.

Feature Number 4

This feature was the first to be found in Area II. It was first noted along the center of the west wall in unit 570-540 and was found to continue for a short distance into the center part of unit 570-550. It was a basin-shaped depression filled with a hard brownish sand. Its maximum east-west measurement was approximately 3 feet at the base of the plow zone. At the same point it had a north-south measurement of 4 feet. The outline was irregular but basically circular. It was only .2 to .3 feet in thickness for most of its area but near the center, in unit 570-540, it reached a depth of 1.6 feet below the surface, or .8 feet below the plow zone. Cultural material and charcoal were very sparse.

Feature Number 5

Feature Number 5 was located in Area III in the southeast quarter of the southeast quarter of unit 570-490 (Figure 3). The center of this feature consisted of an oblong area about 1 foot long and .8 feet deep filled with black and grey ash and sand. This area was surrounded by hard reddish-brown sands which gradually merged with the brownish-yellow sand of the $A_2$ zone.

Feature Number 6

Feature Number 6 was also located in Area II in the south half of unit 570-490. It was distinct from Feature Number 5 but rather close to it and similar in appearance (Figure 3). It was roughly oval and had a maximum north-south measurement of 2.5 feet and an east-west measurement of 4 feet. It was marked by a central area similar to that of Feature Number 5 with black and grey ash, charcoal, and organic material and was surrounded by an area of hard reddish-brown sand which graded into the yellow sand of the rest of the unit. This particular area was riddled with rodent burrows including some which were so recent that the soft fill dirt could easily be worked out with trowels. Two of the burrows could be traced the entire length of the unit. A side-notched projectile point was recovered. Its association with the feature, however, is not certain since it was found in a rodent burrow running through the feature. Yarnell (1964:196) examined this charcoal and identified maple, tamarack, blue beech, and sycamore.

Feature Number 7

Feature Number 7 was in Area I in the corner of excavation units 620-480, 620-470, 630-480 and 630-470. It was first recognized in unit 620-480 where an area of dense charcoal concentration was noted in the northwest corner. This was the central element of the feature. The charcoal concentration lay over the area of white ash which lay over hard reddish-brown sand which, in turn, graded into the yellow and yellowish-brown sands of the site. This feature was traced to a depth of slightly over 2 feet when further excavation was abandoned. Very little cultural material was found and there is little doubt that this was a burned-out tree stump. As with Feature Number 3, Yarnell (1964:198) identified the charcoal from this feature as exclusively beech.

Feature Number 8

Feature Number 8 was located in Area II in the southwest quarter of the southeast quarter of unit 590-540. This was an area where much surface material had been noted. In clearing the plow zone the remnants of a previous excavation unit were uncovered. It was a fairly regular pit 4 feet wide and 7 feet long. It ran to a depth of .3 feet below the plow zone, had steep sides and was filled with the brown sandy loam of the plow zone. Many small chips were found in the fill but they were plentiful over the surface in this area. DeVisscher and Wahla did not know who had opened this unit but it appeared to have been fairly recent. A faint basin-shaped depression was noted to the south of the old excavation which partly cut into it. This area contained cultural material and ran to a depth of .5 feet below the plow zone so it was deeper than the old excavation unit. Whoever opened it had cut into the feature and either not seen it or ignored it in a search for artifacts. The feature was basin-shaped with a maximum north-south measurement of 2 feet and a maximum east-west measurement of 3 feet. The fill was reddish-brown, hard-packed sands which contrasted with the yellow sand of the rest of the unit.

In addition to the above features there are five other places in Area I and one in Area II which look like burned out stumps. These are areas of dense charcoal concentrations, beds of grey ash, and discolored, hardened reddish-brown sand which can be followed to a considerable depth. Several of these were traced to the water table which was about 4 feet below the surface. These were found in the southwest quarter of unit 620-510 and the adjacent 5- by 5-foot unit 615-515, in the north half of unit 620-490 and the south half of 630-490, in the south half of unit 620-470, in the eastern half of 620-470 and the western half of 620-460, in the southwest quarter of unit 630-490 and the southeast quarter of unit 640-490, and in the center of unit 600-540 in Area II.

Four of the features at the site appear to be associated with the main occupation of the site. These are features Number 1, 2, 4, and 8. Two of the features, Numbers 3 and 7, appear to be burned-out stumps, which, when coupled with the unnumbered burned-out stumps, give us a total of eight such occurrences in the area that we excavated. The evidence for the function, or nature, of Features Number 5 and 6 is not conclusive. They form isolated units but differ from the larger group of Paleo-Indian features. They are either hearths of a later occupation or natural disturbances.

In addition to the burned-out stumps there are patches of ash and flecks of charcoal just below the plow zone over much of the site. These, no doubt, are related to the clearing of the land for agriculture. Charred legume nodules were also found at considerable depths. These would have no great antiquity. The site is much too disturbed to get an accurate radiocarbon date on any of the charcoal samples from the site. This was demonstrated by the date obtained on material from Feature Number 3, which we have interpreted as a burned-out tree stump. The date of 1630 B.C. ± 200 (M-1401) means only that some of the charcoal in the sample might have been, at one time, associated with Paleo-Indian hearths, but most of it was not.

The amount of disturbance was also demonstrated by Yarnell (1964:19), who found charcoal from recent forest types well below the plow zone at the site.

# III

## THE HOLCOMBE CHIPPED-STONE INDUSTRY

### The Nature of the Sample

The combined collections of DeVisscher and the University of Michigan Museum of Anthropology provided a total sample of over 8,000 pieces of chipped or fractured stone.* Most of this material was dèbitage which provided the largest and most consistent part of the sample. There were 7,660 fragments of chipped or fractured stone which showed no signs of retouch or use. The DeVisscher collection furnished 2,517 such fragments and the remainder came from the University of Michigan excavation. There were an additional 393 artifacts from the site; 142 were recovered from the University of Michigan excavations and 251 were collected by DeVisscher.

The material used by the Holcombe knappers was predominatly Bayport chert which accounted for 96.9 per cent of the artifacts and 96.1 per cent of the dèbitage. Bayport chert was studied in detail by Fred Dustin who noted that "at least ninety per cent of the arrow-points, drills, perforators, scrapers and cutting blades collected in the Lower Peninsula" were made of this material (Dustin, 1935:471).

The Bayport chert nodules were formed in the Upper Grand Rapids or Bayport limestone formations (Dustin, 1935:466) with outcroppings in Arenac, Huron, and Tuscola Counties. The nodules are small with the vast majority being less than 4 inches in diameter. Dustin reported that nodules 6 inches in diameter were rare and he had seen only two that were 8 inches in diameter. They are marked by a series of concentric lines of formation. Quartz inclusions occur and fossils are frequent.

The Bayport chert is basically grey in color but varies from a white, chalky material found on the outer surface of the nodules, to a dense dark grey often found near the center of the

*DeVisscher made an additional 3,418 flint chips available for study in 1965. These will be discussed in Chapter VIII.

nodules. Dustin (1935:470) has even reported cores of transluscent chalcedony or transparent quartz but these are, at best, small inclusions in the generally grey chert. Most of the material is dull but occasional lustrous examples are found.

For this study, the basic Bayport classification was broken into three subgroups. The first of these subgroups was a white Bayport chert which is usually softer and with a more chalky texture than the darker forms. This is not, however, a universal characteristic and those examples which display this trait may be heavily patinated or made from fragments of cortex. In an earlier study I recognized both white and brown categories (Fitting, 1964*b*: 236). At that time Keslin suggested that the Brown specimens were patinated examples of white cherts. Further experimentation confirmed this and they are grouped in the present study. The color range is, therefore, very large, running from white (Munsell 10 YR, 8/1, 8/2) through very pale brown (Munsell 10 YR, 8/3, 8/4, 7/3, 7/4) to yellow (Munsell 10 YR, 8/6, 8/8, 7/6, 7/8), brownish-yellow (Munsell 10 YR, 6/4, 6/6, 6/8) and yellowish brown (Munsell 10 YR, 5/4, 5/6, 5/8).

The second Bayport group consists of light grey Bayport chert. This is a breakdown of my previous light grey to dark grey grouping brought about by use of Munsell colors (Fitting, 1964*b*:236). It includes the best cherts of the Bayport series. The color range is from light grey (Munsell 10 YR, 7/1, 7/2, 6/1) through grey (Munsell 10 YR, 5/1) to light brownish-grey (Munsell 10 YR, 6/2) and greyish-brown (Munsell 10 YR, 5/2).

The third Bayport category consists of dark grey Bayport cherts. There is some evidence that this darker color may be, in part, a result of heat alteration. Many artifacts and flakes in this group also show evidence of heat spalling. The color range of this group is from dark grey (Munsell 10 YR, 4/1) to very dark grey (Munsell 10 YR, 3/1).

The exotic materials, which form 3 per cent of the total sample, may be further broken down into subgroups. A sample of 210 small flakes out of the 252 exotic specimens was examined in detail. Out of this sample 49 per cent was a distinctive black flint with a high luster, no inclusions, and no fossils. Enough large flakes were found to suggest that this material was obtained in a tabular rather than a nodular form.

There was a closely related series of dark purple or winey flint with a high luster, no inclusions and no fossils which might have come from the same formation as the black flint. It accounted for 24 per cent of the exotic material studied and the two categories combined accounted for 73 per cent of the exotic material. I am inclined to look to Ohio for the source of this material.

Seven per cent of the exotic-looking material consisted of red and pink specimens of a chert which, except for the coloration, fell in the white Bayport chert series. I am of the opinion that this is a white Bayport variant which has been altered and discolored by minerals in the soil at the site.

Four per cent of the sample consisted of a lustrous chert with brown, grey, and olive banding.

Three per cent of the sample consisted of large flakes of green slate. If we had weighed the exotic materials, this percentage would have been higher since the flakes are large. They are the only nonsiliceous material among our exotics. There were also several slate objects among the artifacts which were not included in the sample of the exotic material.

Three per cent of the sample consisted of a light purplish chert with brown flecks and a high luster. Two per cent of the sample consisted of a finely banded olive, white, and red chert; 1 per cent consisted of a milky white flint and the remaining 6 per cent was divided among fourteen unique forms, each of which constituted less than 1 per cent of the sample.

In summarizing the nature of the exotic materials it is clear that most of the exotics have a single outside source and form a consistent group. These black and wine-colored flints make up over 70 per cent of the sample of exotics. The rest of the exotic material could probably be obtained from pebble sources in local drift.

## Débitage

### *Flake and Fracture Types*

In order to study the 7,660 pieces of débitage from the site, the material was divided into four categories of flake and fracture types. Both large flakes of bifacial retouch and small retouch flakes were present (Jelinek:personal communication). The flakes which were the result of bifacial retouch were separated into two classes based on the presence or absence of the striking platform. The fourth category consisted of blocky fragments of chert. Since there is evidence that these resulted from natural alteration rather than purposeful knapping, Jelinek has suggested that the term "block fracture flake" be used to describe them. (See Plate II for flake types.)

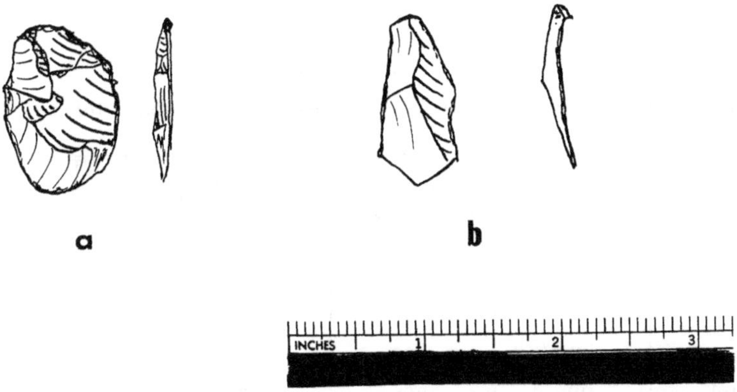


FIG. 4. Flakes of bifacial retouch.

The smallest flake-type category was that of flakes of bifacial retouch with striking platforms (Figure 4) which were struck from bifacial objects, rather than cores, by means of percussion (Jelinek:personal communication). There were 216 such specimens in the sample and their distribution among the several chert categories is given in Table 1. This table is broken into percentages in Table 2 and the total and average weights are given in Table 3.

Out of the total series of 216 a sample of 176 were studied in detail. Expanding flakes (White, 1963:9) accounted for 63 per cent of the sample. In all instances the striking platforms of these expanding flakes formed an acute angle with the outer surface of the flake. Almost all of these, 108 out of 111, showed evidence of either use or grinding along the edge of the striking platform.

Eighteen per cent of the samples studied were parallel flakes (White, 1963:9). These, too, were marked by an acute angle between the striking platform and the outer surface of the flake. Only two out of the thirty-two flakes in this group lacked grinding on the edges.

Another 6 per cent of the samples also had an acute angle between the striking platform and the outer surface as well as ground edges. Most of these were flakes which "feathered out" almost immediately but a few (1 per cent of the sample) consisted of contracting flakes (White, 1963:9). Thus, 88 per cent of the sample was marked by an acute angle between the outer surface of the flake and the striking platform as well as by edge grinding.

TABLE 1

CHERT AND FLAKE TYPES

Numbers of Flakes in the Several Chert Categories among the Dèbitage from the Holcombe Site

| | Bayport White | Bayport Light Grey | Bayport Dark Grey | Exotic | Total |
|---|---|---|---|---|---|
| Flakes with striking platforms . . | 71 | 81 | 36 | 28 | 216 |
| Flakes without striking platforms . . | 76 | 95 | 70 | 43 | 284 |
| Block fracture flakes . | 220 | 289 | 568 | 4 | 1081 |
| Small retouch flakes . . | 1570 | 2797 | 1537 | 175 | 6079 |
| Total . . . . . . . . . | 1937 | 3262 | 2211 | 250 | 7660 |

TABLE 2

CHERT AND FLAKE TYPES

Percentages of Flakes in the Several Chert Categories among the Dèbitage from the Holcombe Site

| | Bayport White | Bayport Light Grey | Bayport Dark Grey | Exotic | Total |
|---|---|---|---|---|---|
| Flakes with striking platforms . . | .9 | 1.1 | .5 | .4 | 2.8 |
| Flakes without striking platforms . . | 1.0 | 1.2 | .9 | .6 | 3.7 |
| Block fracture flakes . | 2.9 | 3.8 | 7.4 | .1 | 14.1 |
| Small retouch flakes . . | 20.5 | 36.5 | 20.1 | 2.3 | 79.4 |
| Total . . . . . . . . . | 25.3 | 42.5 | 28.9 | 3.3 | 100.0 |

Six per cent of the samples were very heavy flakes with a right angle between the striking platform and the outer surface of the flake. These flakes might have been manufactured by a block-on-block technique and show little evidence of controlled percussion. The remaining 6 per cent consisted of large channel flakes removed in the process of fluting the points from the site. Many of the small retouch flakes were obviously the result of basal thinning of projectile points but these flakes demonstrate that true fluting was being carried on at the site.

There were 284 thin flakes from the site which have been classified as flakes of bifacial retouch without striking platforms. They are similar to the last group except that they lack striking platforms. The chert classification for these flakes is given in Table 1, the percentages in Table 2 and the total and average weights in Table 3. The fact that they weigh less than the flakes of bifacial retouch with striking platforms, .66 grams as opposed to .78 grams, suggests that some are fragments of larger flakes which originally had striking platforms but were later broken. Although it cannot be demonstrated, it is probable that this series, like those with striking platforms, is a product of percussion flaking.

The third group of flakes from the site was a series of 6,079 small retouch flakes which were probably a product of pressure retouch. The chert distribution for this group is given in Table 1, the percentage of the total dèbitage in Table 2 and the total and average weights in Table 3. Numerically, this is the largest single category and accounts for more than 79 per cent of the dèbitage. On the other hand, the small size of individual retouch flakes means that they account for only 33 per cent of the sample by weight. The average weight of these flakes is only .09 grams for the entire site so their small size can be readily visualized. This factor had to be taken into account for all statistical comparisons since tests based on count alone would be biased toward small retouch flakes.

TABLE 3

COUNTS AND WEIGHTS OF FLAKES

Counts, Percentages, Weight in Grams of Total Sample of Flakes, Percentage of Total Weight for Each Flake Category and Average Weight of Flakes in Each Category Given in Grams

| | N | Per cent N | Weight | Per cent Weight | Average Weight |
|---|---|---|---|---|---|
| Flakes with striking platforms . . . . . . . . . | 216 | 2.8 | 167.5 | 9.9 | .78 |
| Flakes without striking platforms . . . | 284 | 3.7 | 188.2 | 11.1 | .66 |
| Block fracture flakes . . | 1081 | 14.1 | 781.1 | 46.0 | .72 |
| Small retouch flakes . . . | 6079 | 79.4 | 559.9 | 33.0 | .09 |
| Total . . . . . . . . . . | 7660 | 100.0 | 1696.7 | 100.0 | |

The final category is that of block fracture flakes. There are 1,081 pieces of dèbitage classed with this group. The surfaces of cleavage are right angled or at acute angles to each other. There are usually several such surfaces on a fragment. There is no evidence of a striking platform, a bulb of percussion, or ripples of percussion on these specimens. It is possible that some of these were not a product of knapping but were formed by heat fracture which may occur at a lower temperature than that causing spalling. Evidence for this position will be presented in a separate section of this study. The count and chert distribution of this category is presented in Table 1, the percentages in Table 2 and the total and average weights in Table 3. Because the size of block fracture flakes more closely corresponds to that of flakes of bifacial retouch these groups can be quantitatively compared.

### *Correlation of Chert and Flake Types*

From looking at the distribution of flake types and chert types in Tables 1 and 2 it becomes apparent that the greatest discrepancy is in the category of block fracture flakes. The frequency of block fracture flakes in the dark grey Bayport category is very high and the number of exotic block fracture flakes is very low.

The significance of this association was tested in several ways. First, the chert, flakes of bifacial retouch, and block fracture flakes were plotted against each other and tested by the chi-square technique (Table 4). Our hypothesis was that there is no difference between the observed and expected distributions. The resulting chi-square value, 249.42, was extremely high and the difference was highly significant. The $\phi^2$ value used to measure the strength of relationship was also relatively high. Therefore, we cannot accept the hypothesis that there is no difference in the two distributions.

This was again tested using dark grey block fracture flakes and comparing them with all other flake and chert types grouped (Table 5). The hypothesis was the same and an even higher value for chi-square was obtained although the strength of relationship, as measured by $\phi^2$, was lower. In both instances there is less than one chance in a thousand that the observed discrepancies are caused by chance alone. There seems to be a strong positive association between block fracture flakes and dark grey Bayport chert and a corresponding negative association between exotic material and block fracture flakes.

TABLE 4

CHERT AND FLAKE TYPES

Chi-square Test of Chert and Flake Type Association Showing the Large Number of Block Fracture Flakes Which Occur on Dark Grey Bayport Chert and Its Level of Significance

| | Bayport White | | Bayport Light Grey | | Bayport Dark Grey | | Exotic | | Total |
|---|---|---|---|---|---|---|---|---|---|
| | Obs. | Expt. | Obs. | Expt. | Obs. | Expt. | Obs. | Expt. | |
| Flakes with striking platforms . . . | 71 | 50 | 84 | 64 | 36 | 92 | 38 | 10 | 216 |
| Flakes without striking platforms . . . | 76 | 66 | 95 | 83 | 70 | 121 | 43 | 13 | 284 |
| Block fracture flakes. . . . . . | 220 | 251 | 289 | 318 | 568 | 461 | 4 | 52 | 1081 |
| Total . . . . | 367 | | 468 | | 674 | | 75 | | 1581 |

$\chi^2 = 249.42$ df = 6 $p < .001$

$\phi^2 = .158$

TABLE 5

BLOCK FRACTURE FLAKES ON DARK GREY BAYPORT CHERT COMPARED WITH ALL OTHER CHERT AND FLAKE TYPES

Observed and Expected Frequencies of Block Fracture Flakes on Dark Grey Bayport Chert Compared to all other Flake and Fracture Types with the Results of the Chi-square Test

| | Dark Grey Bayport Chert | | All Other Cherts | | Total |
|---|---|---|---|---|---|
| | Observed | Expected | Observed | Expected | |
| Block fracture flakes . . | 568 | 298 | 513 | 783 | 1081 |
| All other flake types . . . | 1643 | 1913 | 4936 | 5666 | 6579 |
| Total . . . . . . . . . . | 2211 | | 5449 | | 7660 |

$\chi^2 = 392.46$ df = 1 $p < .001$

$\phi^2 = .051$

## *Comparison Between the DeVisscher Collection and the University of Michigan Collection*

While counting and weighing the dèbitage I had the impression that there were distinct differences between the University of Michigan sample and the material which was collected by DeVisscher. This might be expected in light of the differences in sampling technique; surface collection as opposed to screened excavations.

Several chi-square tests were run to compare the two collections. The flakes of bifacial retouch and block fracture flakes are compared in Table 6. Our null hypothesis is that there is no difference between the observed and expected distribution of flake types in the two collections. Because of the high chi-square value, and the relatively high $\phi^2$ value, we cannot accept our hypothesis. The big discrepancy here is between the observed and expected numbers of flakes of bifacial retouch without striking platforms.

The weights of these flake groups were also tested (Table 7) and significant differences were again noted. The cause was again the greater weight of the flakes of bifacial retouch in the University of Michigan collections.

TABLE 6

COMPARISON OF LARGE FLAKES IN THE UNIVERSITY OF MICHIGAN COLLECTION AND THE DEVISSCHER COLLECTION

Observed and Expected Frequencies of Flakes of Bifacial Workmanship, and Block Fracture Flakes in the University of Michigan Museum of Anthropology (UMMA) and DeVisscher Collection with the Results of the Chi-square Test

| | UMMA Collection | | DeVisscher Collection | | Total |
|---|---|---|---|---|---|
| | Observed | Expected | Observed | Expected | |
| Flakes with striking platforms . . . . . . . . . | 90 | 140 | 126 | 76 | 216 |
| Flakes without striking platforms . . . . . . . . . | 215 | 184 | 69 | 100 | 284 |
| Block fracture flakes . . | 721 | 702 | 360 | 379 | 1081 |
| Total . . . . . . . . . . | 1026 | | 555 | | 1581 |

$\chi^2 = 67.05$ df = 2 $p < .001$

$\phi^2 = .042$

TABLE 7

COMPARISON OF LARGE FLAKES IN THE UNIVERSITY OF MICHIGAN COLLECTION AND THE DEVISSCHER COLLECTION

Observed and Expected Total Weights in Grams of Flakes of Bifacial Workmanship and Block Fracture Flakes in the University of Michigan Museum of Anthropology (UMMA) and DeVisscher Collections with the Results of the Chi-square Test

| | UMMA Collection | | DeVisscher Collection | | Total |
|---|---|---|---|---|---|
| | Observed | Expected | Observed | Expected | |
| Flakes with striking platforms . . . . . . . . | 79 | 101 | 89 | 67 | 168 |
| Flakes without striking platforms . . . . . . . . | 131 | 113 | 58 | 76 | 189 |
| Block fracture flakes . | 471 | 467 | 310 | 314 | 781 |
| Total . . . . . . . . . | 681 | | 457 | | 1138 |

$\chi^2 = 19.23$ df = 2 $p < .001$

$\phi^2 = .017$

TABLE 8

AVERAGE WEIGHTS OF LARGE FLAKES IN THE UNIVERSITY OF MICHIGAN COLLECTION AND THE DEVISSCHER COLLECTION

Average Weight in Grams of Flakes of Bifacial Workmanship and Block Fracture Flakes in the University of Michigan Museum of Anthropology (UMMA) and DeVisscher Collections

| | UMMA Collection | DeVisscher Collection |
|---|---|---|
| Flakes with striking platforms . . . . . . . . . . . . | .60 | .97 |
| Flakes without striking platforms . . . . . . . . . . . . | .58 | .76 |
| Block fracture flakes . . . . . | .65 | .86 |

The explanation for this might be that DeVisscher tended to pick up the more obviously worked or more readily visable flakes to the neglect of the smaller and less obviously worked flakes. This was demonstrated by the relative weights of flakes of bifacial retouch and block fracture flakes in the two collections

(Table 8). All flake types are lighter in the University of Michigan collection. There is only a .02 gram difference between the flakes of bifacial retouch with striking platforms and those without striking platforms in the University collections while there is a .21 gram difference between these groups in the DeVisscher collection.

The relative frequencies of the several chert groups among the flakes of bifacial retouch and block fracture flakes were also tested (Table 9). There was no significant difference between the observed and expected frequencies of chert types among the large flake groups. This much variation would be expected between 20 and 30 per cent of the time by chance alone.

There was, however, a significant difference between cherts among the small retouch flakes in the two collections (Table 10). This was somewhat confusing because there was no significant difference between the weights of the chert groups for the small retouch flakes in the two collections (Table 11). The difference can be explained by comparing the weights of the two collections of small retouch flakes. The average weight of small retouch flakes in the University collection was .10 grams while the average weight of a small retouch flake in the DeVisscher collection was .07 grams. This also reflects sampling procedure. The

TABLE 9

COMPARISON OF LARGE FLAKE CHERT TYPES IN THE UNIVERSITY OF MICHIGAN AND DEVISSCHER COLLECTIONS

Observed and Expected Frequencies of Chert Types among the Large Flake Types in the University of Michigan and DeVisscher Collections with the Results of the Chi-square Test

| | UMMA Collection | | DeVisscher Collection | | Total |
|---|---|---|---|---|---|
| | Observed | Expected | Observed | Expected | |
| White Bayport...... | 235 | 238 | 132 | 129 | 367 |
| Light grey Bayport... | 288 | 302 | 177 | 163 | 465 |
| Dark grey Bayport... | 456 | 437 | 218 | 237 | 674 |
| Exotic........... | 47 | 49 | 28 | 26 | 75 |
| Total......... | 1026 | | 555 | | 1581 |

$\chi^2 = 4.54$ df = 3 $p < .30$

$\phi^2 = .003$

TABLE 10

COMPARISON OF RETOUCH FLAKE CHERT TYPES IN THE UNIVERSITY OF MICHIGAN AND DEVISSCHER COLLECTIONS

Observed and Expected Frequencies of Chert Types among the Small Retouch Flakes in the University of Michigan and DeVisscher Collections with the Results of the Chi-square Test

| | UMMA Collection | | DeVisscher Collection | | Total |
|---|---|---|---|---|---|
| | Observed | Expected | Observed | Expected | |
| White Bayport . . . . . . | 1123 | 1063 | 447 | 507 | 1570 |
| Light grey Bayport. . . | 1858 | 1894 | 939 | 903 | 2797 |
| Dark grey Bayport . . . | 1007 | 1041 | 530 | 496 | 1537 |
| Exotic . . . . . . . . . . . | 129 | 119 | 46 | 56 | 175 |
| Total . . . . . . . . . | 4117 | | 1962 | | 6079 |

$\chi^2 = 18.94$ df = 3 $p < .001$

$\phi^2 = .003$

TABLE 11

COMPARISON OF RETOUCH FLAKE CHERT TYPES IN THE UNIVERSITY OF MICHIGAN AND DEVISSCHER COLLECTIONS

Observed and Expected Weights in Grams of Chert Types among the Small Retouch Flakes in the University of Michigan and DeVisscher Collections with the Results of the Chi-square Test

| | UMMA Collection | | DeVisscher Collection | | Total |
|---|---|---|---|---|---|
| | Observed | Expected | Observed | Expected | |
| White Bayport . . . . . . . | 112 | 109 | 34 | 37 | 146 |
| Light grey Bayport . . . | 191 | 192 | 66 | 65 | 257 |
| Dark grey Bayport . . . . | 102 | 104 | 37 | 35 | 139 |
| Exotic . . . . . . . . . . . . | 14 | 13 | 4 | 5 | 18 |
| Total . . . . . . . . . . | 419 | | 141 | | 560 |

$\chi^2 = .78$ df = 3 $p < .90$

$\phi^2 = .001$

University excavators used a quarter-inch screen and lost most of the smaller retouch flakes which fell through the screen. DeVisscher saved retouch flakes of all sizes so the average weight of small retouch flakes in his collection is much less.

All of these differences lead to a conclusion that the two collections are not directly comparable. DeVisscher picked up larger flakes of bifacial retouch and smaller small retouch flakes than were recovered in the University screens. The difference is also shown in the ratio of artifacts to dèbitage in the two collections. DeVisscher collected one artifact for every ten pieces of dèbitage while there is only one artifact for every forty pieces of dèbitage in the University of Michigan collection. Therefore, to eliminate the possibility of collection bias causing errors, comparisons of dèbitage from excavated areas will be made only with other excavated areas rather than the entire sample.

### *An Examination of Block Fracture Flakes*

Before proceeding, it might be profitable to examine the areas of the site where block fracture flakes were recovered and present the evidence for our interpretation of this material as having been fractured by heat.

The association between block fractures and dark grey chert was suspicious so we watched for other associations. One such association was found during our examination of fire-cracked rock from the site. Fire-cracked rock, granitic rock with evidence of fractures caused by temperature change, was not abundant on the site. There were only 125 pieces of fire-cracked rock recovered in the course of excavation. They had a total weight of 683.1 grams and an average weight of 5.5 grams. Altogether, there were 47 provenience units, including levels within excavation units, which produced this material.

It seems logical to assume that provenience units with fire-cracked rock were in, or near, fired areas and the dèbitage in these units was also in, or near, fired areas. In Table 12 we have compared the flakes of bifacial workmanship and block fracture flakes from provenience units with fire-cracked rock and provenience units without fire-cracked rock. When this was tested by the chi-square technique, with a null hypothesis that there was no difference between the two groups, we found we could not accept the hypothesis. The discrepancy was so large as to arise less than one chance in a thousand if chance alone were affecting

TABLE 12

UNITS WITH FIRE-CRACKED ROCK AND FLAKE TYPES

Observed and Expected Numbers of Flakes of Bifacial Retouch and Block Fracture Flakes Found in Provenience Units with Fire-cracked Rock and Provenience Units without Fire-cracked Rock with the Results of the Chi-square Test on these Values

| | Provenience units with Fire-cracked Rock | | Provenience units without Fire-cracked Rock | | Total |
|---|---|---|---|---|---|
| | Observed | Expected | Observed | Expected | |
| Flakes with striking platforms . . . . . . . . | 50 | 49 | 40 | 41 | 90 |
| Flakes without striking platforms . . . . . . . . | 82 | 116 | 133 | 99 | 215 |
| Block fracture flakes . | 422 | 399 | 299 | 322 | 721 |
| Total . . . . . . . . . | 554 | | 472 | | 1026 |

$\chi^2 = 27.80$ df = 2 $p < .001$

$\phi^2 = .027$

the distribution. It was caused by a dearth of flakes of bifacial retouch and an abundance of block fracture flakes in provenience units with fire-cracked rock. The phi-square value is also relatively high.

In Table 13 the comparison of small retouch flakes and all other flake categories combined is given for the two groups of provenience units. This was tested in the same manner and the descrepancy between the observed and expected values was so large that it would occur less than one time in a thousand by chance alone. The reason for the high value of chi-square was the low frequency of small retouch flakes in provenience units with fire-cracked rock. The phi-square value here is very low, however, so this test can only be used to supplement tests with stronger relationships.

Using the same division between provenience units with fire-cracked rock and those without fire-cracked rock, we plotted the frequencies of chert types from the site (Table 14). This too was tested by chi-square and the results were highly significant. The units with fire-cracked rock produced less than the expected frequency of white and light grey Bayport cherts and more than the expected frequency of dark grey and exotic materials.

With this information in mind, I decided to examine the

TABLE 13

UNITS WITH FIRE-CRACKED ROCK AND FLAKE TYPES

Observed and Expected Numbers of Small Retouch Flakes and all other Types of Flakes Found in Provenience Units with Fire-cracked Rock and Provenience Units without Fire-cracked Rock with the Results of the Chi-square Test on these Values

| | Provenience units with Fire-cracked Rock | | Provenience units without Fire-cracked Rock | | Total |
|---|---|---|---|---|---|
| | Observed | Expected | Observed | Expected | |
| Small retouch flakes . . . | 554 | 507 | 472 | 519 | 1026 |
| Other flake types . . . . . | 1987 | 2034 | 2130 | 2083 | 4117 |
| Total . . . . . . . . . . | 2541 | | 2602 | | 5143 |

$\chi^2 = 10.76$ df = 1 $p < .01$

$\phi^2 = .002$

TABLE 14

UNITS WITH FIRE-CRACKED ROCK AND CHERT TYPE

Observed and Expected Frequencies of the Four Chert Classifications Found in Provenience Units with Fire-cracked Rock and Provenience Units without Fire-cracked Rock with the Results of the Chi-square Test on these Values

| | Provenience units with Fire-cracked Rock | | Provenience units without Fire-cracked Rock | | Total |
|---|---|---|---|---|---|
| | Observed | Expected | Observed | Expected | |
| White Bayport . . . . . . | 660 | 671 | 698 | 687 | 1358 |
| Light grey Bayport. . . | 1003 | 1060 | 1143 | 1086 | 2146 |
| Dark grey Bayport . . . | 763 | 723 | 700 | 740 | 1463 |
| Exotic materials . . . . | 115 | 87 | 61 | 89 | 176 |
| Total . . . . . . . . . | 2541 | | 2602 | | 5143 |

$\chi^2 = 26.67$ df = 3 $p < .001$

$\phi^2 = .005$

TABLE 15

FEATURES AND FLAKE TYPES

Observed and Expected Numbers of Flakes of Bifacial Retouch and Block Fracture Flakes from Features and Other Areas on the Site with the Chi-square Test on these Values

| | Features | | Other Areas | | Total |
|---|---|---|---|---|---|
| | Observed | Expected | Observed | Expected | |
| Flakes with striking platforms . . . . . . . . | 2 | 9 | 88 | 81 | 90 |
| Flakes without striking platforms . . . . . . . . | 22 | 22 | 193 | 193 | 215 |
| Block fracture flakes . | 80 | 73 | 641 | 648 | 721 |
| Total . . . . . . . . . | 104 | | 922 | | 1026 |

$\chi^2 = 6.80$ df = 2 $p < .05$

$\phi^2 = .007$

contents of features in relation to other areas of the site. All of the features, whether natural or cultural, were caused by fire action of some sort; therefore, the same associations would be expected.

In Table 15 all of the flakes of bifacial retouch and block fracture flakes from features were compared to the material from other excavated areas on the site. The difference between the observed and expected frequencies was so large that we would expect it less than one time in twenty if chance alone were operating. This is a significant, but not a highly significant, difference. There is also a low phi-square value.

There is some inconsistency between this distribution and that observed in the provenience units with fire-cracked rock. The former had the expected numbers of flakes of bifacial retouch with striking platforms and fewer than the expected numbers of flakes of bifacial retouch without striking platforms. The features had the expected numbers of flakes of bifacial retouch without striking platforms and fewer than the expected number with striking platforms. Both provenience units with fire-cracked rock and features were consistent in having greater than expected numbers of block fracture flakes.

The frequencies of chert groups were also tested for features and areas outside of features at the site (Table 16). Here the chi-square value is very high and the difference between the observed and expected distributions is highly significant. The phi-square value is relatively high.

TABLE 16

FEATURES AND CHERT TYPES

Observed and Expected Numbers of the Four Chert Classifications Found in Features and Other Areas with the Results of the Chi-square Test on these Values

| | Features | | Other Areas | | Total |
|---|---|---|---|---|---|
| | Observed | Expected | Observed | Expected | |
| White Bayport...... | 79 | 145 | 1279 | 1213 | 1358 |
| Light grey Bayport... | 270 | 228 | 1876 | 1918 | 2146 |
| Dark grey Bayport ... | 190 | 156 | 1273 | 1307 | 1463 |
| Exotic material..... | 9 | 19 | 167 | 157 | 176 |
| Total......... | 548 | | 4595 | | 5143 |

$\chi^2 = 56.48$ df = 3 $p < .001$

$\phi^2 = .011$

There is some inconsistency in the relative frequencies of white and light grey Bayport chert and exotic materials in the units with fire-cracked rock and features at the site. In both cases, however, we have greater than expected frequencies of dark grey Bayport chert in the groups associated with fired area.

Only one feature on the site contained more than 100 pieces of dèbitage. This was Feature Number 2 which contained 143 pieces. Three flakes of bifacial retouch without striking platforms were recovered and the rest of the dèbitage was almost evenly divided between block fracture flakes and small retouch flakes (Table 17). These flakes were compared with the corresponding categories from the rest of the site and the observed and expected distributions were tested by chi-square. The difference was highly significant, with a relatively high measure of strength relationship, and again caused by the high frequency of block fracture flakes in this feature.

The chert distribution in Feature Number 2 was also tested against that in the rest of the site (Table 18). Here the difference between the observed and expected distributions was not

TABLE 17

FEATURE NUMBER 2 AND FLAKE TYPES

Observed and Expected Numbers of Block Fracture Flakes and Small Retouch Flakes Found in Feature Number 2 and all other Excavated Areas of the Site with the Results of the Chi-square Test on these Values

| | Feature Number 2 | | Other Areas | | Total |
|---|---|---|---|---|---|
| | Observed | Expected | Observed | Expected | |
| Block fracture flakes . . | 68 | 21 | 563 | 700 | 721 |
| Small retouch flakes . . . | 71 | 118 | 4046 | 3999 | 4117 |
| Total . . . . . . . . . . | 139 | | 4699 | | 4838 |

$\chi^2 = 127.62$ df = 1 $p < .001$

$\phi^2 = .026$

TABLE 18

FEATURE NUMBER 2 AND CHERT TYPES

Observed and Expected Numbers of the Four Chert Classifications Found in Feature Number 2 and all other Excavated Areas of the Site with the Results of the Chi-square Test on these Values

| | Feature Number 2 | | Other Areas | | Total |
|---|---|---|---|---|---|
| | Observed | Expected | Observed | Expected | |
| White Bayport . . . . . . . | 30 | 38 | 1328 | 1320 | 1358 |
| Light grey Bayport. . . . | 43 | 41 | 2103 | 2105 | 2146 |
| Dark grey Bayport . . . . | 69 | 60 | 1395 | 1404 | 1464 |
| Exotic material . . . . . . | 1 | 5 | 175 | 171 | 176 |
| Total . . . . . . . . . . | 143 | | 5000 | | 5143 |

$\chi^2 = 6.31$ df = 3 $p < .10$

$\phi^2 = .001$

significant. The relatively high chi-square value ($p < .10$), however, was caused by the high occurrence of dark grey Bayport chert in the feature.

We have consistant associations between fired areas on the site and both block fracture flakes and dark grey Bayport chert. In spite of the weakness of many individual associations they are consistant when taken as a group. This has led to the conclusion that many block fractures are a result of the application of heat short of the required temperature for spalling and that the dark grey color on many flakes may be a product of heat alteration. Part of this was validated experimentally when I heated Bayport chert according to directions furnished by Don Crabtree (personal communication) and found that each band darkened approximately one Munsell shade after twelve hours of heating and twelve hours of cooling in a sand matrix. Further experimental work is being done on heat alteration of Bayport chert in an attempt to duplicate the block fracture pattern which we have observed here.

## Artifacts from the Holcombe Site

There were 393 chipped-stone artifacts recovered from the Holcombe site by DeVisscher and the University of Michigan crew. The vast majority of these are attributed to the Paleo-Indian occupation of the site. There are 8 non-Paleo-Indian chipped-stone artifacts from the site. Six of these form a rather uniform group of side-notched projectile points (Figure 5,*a-e*, Plate III, *a-e* ) for which the metric data and chert types are listed in Table 19. There was 1 complete bifurcate-stemmed point from the site which was illustrated in another article (Fitting, 1964 : 93) and a base of second bifurcate-stemmed point which is almost identical to the first one. All of these artifacts, with the exception of the point in the rodent burrow in Feature Number 6, came from the surface of the site. The 3 points collected by the University of Michigan came from the area of the fence or in the south field.

The Paleo-Indian artifacts have been divided into three groups for this study. Each group, in turn, has a number of subgroups which include a group of 5 possible cores and core fragments (Group I); a group of 318 bifacially worked artifacts (Group II); and a group of 62 unifacially worked artifacts (Group III). There are 5 bifacial artifacts which were broken and reworked into tool types usually found as unifaces. These artifacts will be described in both groups although they are counted with the bifaces. These three groups of artifacts will be dealt with in turn.

### Group I

Group I consists of 4 possible core fragments and 1 small object which might have been a core. The core fragments are

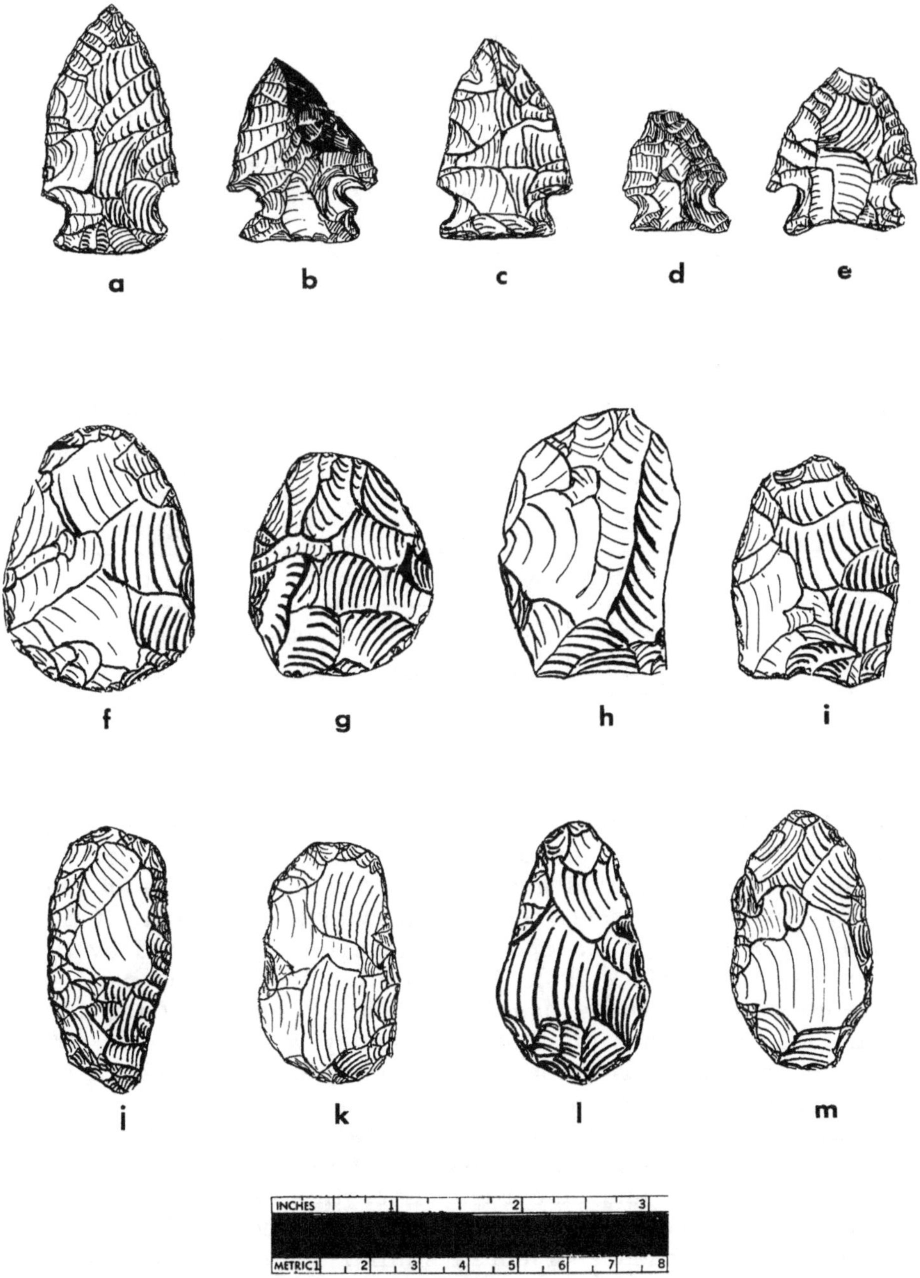


FIG. 5. Artifacts from the Holcombe site. *a-e*, side-notched points; *f-i*, Type A preforms; *j-m*, Type B preforms.

TABLE 19

NON-PALEO-INDIAN PROJECTILE POINTS

Metric and Nonmetric Attributes of Side-notched and Bifurcate-stemmed Points from the Holcombe Site

| Cat. No. | Length (In cm.) | Width | Thick-ness | Hafting Width | Chert | Provenience |
|---|---|---|---|---|---|---|
| Side-notched Points | | | | | | |
| 58013. . . | 2.5 | 1.8 | .6 | 1.2 | dark grey | Feature No. 6 |
| 58018. . . | 3.5 | 3.0 | .7 | 1.8 | light grey | general surface |
| 58018. . . | . . . | 2.8 | 1.0 | 1.6 | dark grey | general surface |
| 58018. . . | . . . | 1.8 | .5 | 1.0 | white | general surface |
| D362 . . . | 5.3 | 2.9 | .8 | 2.2 | white | general surface |
| D361XA . | 5.2 | 2.7 | .9 | 1.7 | light grey | general surface |
| D36A100. | 4.4 | 2.7 | .8 | 1.8 | dark grey | general surface |
| Bifurcate-stemmed Points | | | | | | |
| D368 . . . | . . . | . . . | .4 | 1.1 | light grey | general surface |
| D36 . . . | 2.7 | 1.9 | .4 | 1.1 | dark grey | general surface |

all rather amorphous and of the poorest quality white Bayport chert. It is possible that they are extremely crude Type A preforms. All of these fragments came from DeVissher's collection.

The fifth item in this group may be a bipolar core of dark grey Bayport chert. It is from DeVisscher's collection. If this is a core it would be of the opposing ridge type described by Binford and Quimby (1963: 293). It is similar to what the old world archaeologists call *pièce esquille*. The consensus of the 1964 Les Eyzies conference on lithic technology was that these objects were probably not cores but were possibly used as wedges for splitting bone (Jelinek: personnal communication).

I wish to emphasize that we are dealing with a total sample from the site and there is no possibility that cores were not recognized as such and discarded. Everything from the site over a quarter of an inch in diameter, and much under this dimension, was saved. The absence of cores similar to those found on other Paleo-Indian sites is striking and could not be related to sampling error.

Group II

Group II consists of bifacially worked artifacts. There are 318 artifacts in this group and it is the largest class of artifacts from the site. These bifaces fall into four subgroups. The first two subgroups are composed of varieties of preforms. The term "preform" was used by the 1964 Les Eyzies conference to describe artifacts which represent an intermediate stage in manufacture (Jelinek: personnel communication). These are artifacts which are still generalized and have not taken on the characteristics of finished tools. They are characterized by the almost exclusive use of percussion flaking. They generally do not show signs of use and wear. What alteration is found is usually preparatory to the next stage of manufacture. The term preform is used in preference to the term "blank" since many objects described in the literature as blanks are actually finished tools.

Subgroup A. Type A preforms. Five complete artifacts, eight fragments.

This group of preforms (Figure 5, *f-i*, Plate III, *f-i*) is larger and cruder in appearance than the other bifacial artifacts. The flake scars are massive and parallel to expanding, with the latter predominating. The entire sample of Type A preforms are made from white Bayport chert which is heavily altered and of the poorest quality material in the Bayport series.

One fairly consistant characteristic was the presence of heavy grinding on the edges which was present on 3 of the 5 complete specimens and 7 of the 8 fragmentary examples. I believe that this heavy grinding is correlated with the high frequency of ground edges on flakes of bifacial retouch which have the remnants of their striking platforms. These flakes, like the scars on Type A preforms, are also parallel to expanding with the latter predominating.

Several complete Type A preforms are illustrated in Figure 5, *f-i*, Plate III, *f-i*, and the metric and nonmetric attributes are given in Table 20. The only attribute, besides edge grinding and chert type, which was recorded for the fragments was thickness. The mean of the entire Type A preform sample was 11.31 centimeters and its standard deviation was 2.02 centimeters.

Subgroup B. Type B preforms. Five complete artifacts, 36 end fragments, 10 medial fragments, 56 other fragments.

The Type B preforms differ from the Type A preforms in several respects. They are smaller and lighter than the Type A

TABLE 20

TYPE A PREFORMS

Metric and Nonmetric Attributes of Complete Type A Preforms

| Cat. No. | Length (In cm.) | Width | Thickness | Grinding | Chert | Provenience |
|---|---|---|---|---|---|---|
| 58104. . | 5.6 | 3.3 | 1.1 | no | white | |
| D3628. . | 4.0 | 3.2 | 1.6 | no | white | general surface |
| D3631. . | 4.8 | 3.2 | 1.0 | yes | white | general surface |
| D36 . . . | 5.6 | 3.8 | 1.1 | yes | white | general surface |
| D36 . . . | 5.0 | 3.8 | 1.1 | yes | white | general surface |

TABLE 21

ASSOCIATION OF CHERT TYPE AND EDGE FRAGMENTS

Association of Chert Type and Edge Fragments of Type B Preforms from the Holcombe Site Showing a Highly Significant Value for Chi-square

| | Dark Grey Bayport | | Other Material | |
|---|---|---|---|---|
| | Observed | Expected | Observed | Expected |
| Edge fragments . . . . . . | 32 | 23 | 24 | 33 |
| Other classes . . . . . . . | 11 | 20 | 40 | 31 |

$\chi^2 = 12.63$ df = 1 $p < .001$

$\phi^2 = .118$

TABLE 22

TYPE B PREFORMS

Metric and Nonmetric Attributes of Complete Type B Preforms

| Cat. No. | Length (In cm.) | Width | Thickness | Chert | Provenience |
|---|---|---|---|---|---|
| 57987. . | 5.5 | 3.0 | .8 | white | 610 - 490 |
| 58108. . | 5.5 | 2.5 | .8 | light grey | 630 - 500 |
| D36A67. | 5.0 | 2.6 | 1.3 | light grey | general surface |
| D36D . . | 5.5 | 3.0 | .9 | exotic | general surface |
| D36 . . . | 5.4 | 2.8 | 1.0 | white | general surface |

preforms, the flake scars are not as massive, they are more standardized (Figure 5, *j-m*, Plate III, *j-m*) and the complete examples lack grinding on the edges.

Out of a total sample of 107 Type B preforms and fragments only 15 have traces of grinding on the edges which is found on 7 of the 36 end fragments, three of the 10 medial fragments and only 5 of the 56 edge fragments. I believe that the Type B preforms are made on Type A preforms or, to phrase this in another way, Type B preforms are an intermediate stage between Type A preforms and the finished artifacts. The edges of Type A preforms are apparently ground in the preparation of the striking platform for a percussion blow. Type B preforms are not ground since they are finished and made into tools by means of pressure flaking. The percentage of grinding on broken Type B preforms might indicate breakage during the final stage of percussion flaking.

The chert distribution within this series is also interesting. The chert distribution for the entire series of Type B preforms is as follows: 31 white Bayport, 31 light grey Bayport, 43 dark grey Bayport and two exotic. This distribution is deceptive because 32 of the 43 examples of dark grey Bayport chert are small fragments which would be classed as block flakes except for the traces of bifacial working found on the edges. We might also note that 32 of the 56 small edge fragments are dark grey Bayport chert so we have the same high positive correlation between chert type and flake type noted in the study of the chippage from the site. A chi-square test demonstrating the significance of this association is given in Table 21.

Table 22 shows the metric attributes of the five complete Type B preforms. The only metric attribute which was recorded on the fragments of Type B preforms was thickness. The 5 complete Type B preforms and medial fragments have a mean of 8.06 centimeters and a standard deviation of 1.76 centimeters.

Subgroup C. Finished bifacial artifacts. Six complete projectile points, 102 fragments of projectile point bases, 10 point tips, 23 convergent tips, 20 medial fragments, 23 edge fragments.

As mentioned before (Fitting, 1964*b*: 231), the most numerous class of artifacts from the site were projectile points and point bases (Figures 6-8, Plates IV-VI). In 1962 while I was preparing a preliminary report on the points and bases I had available a

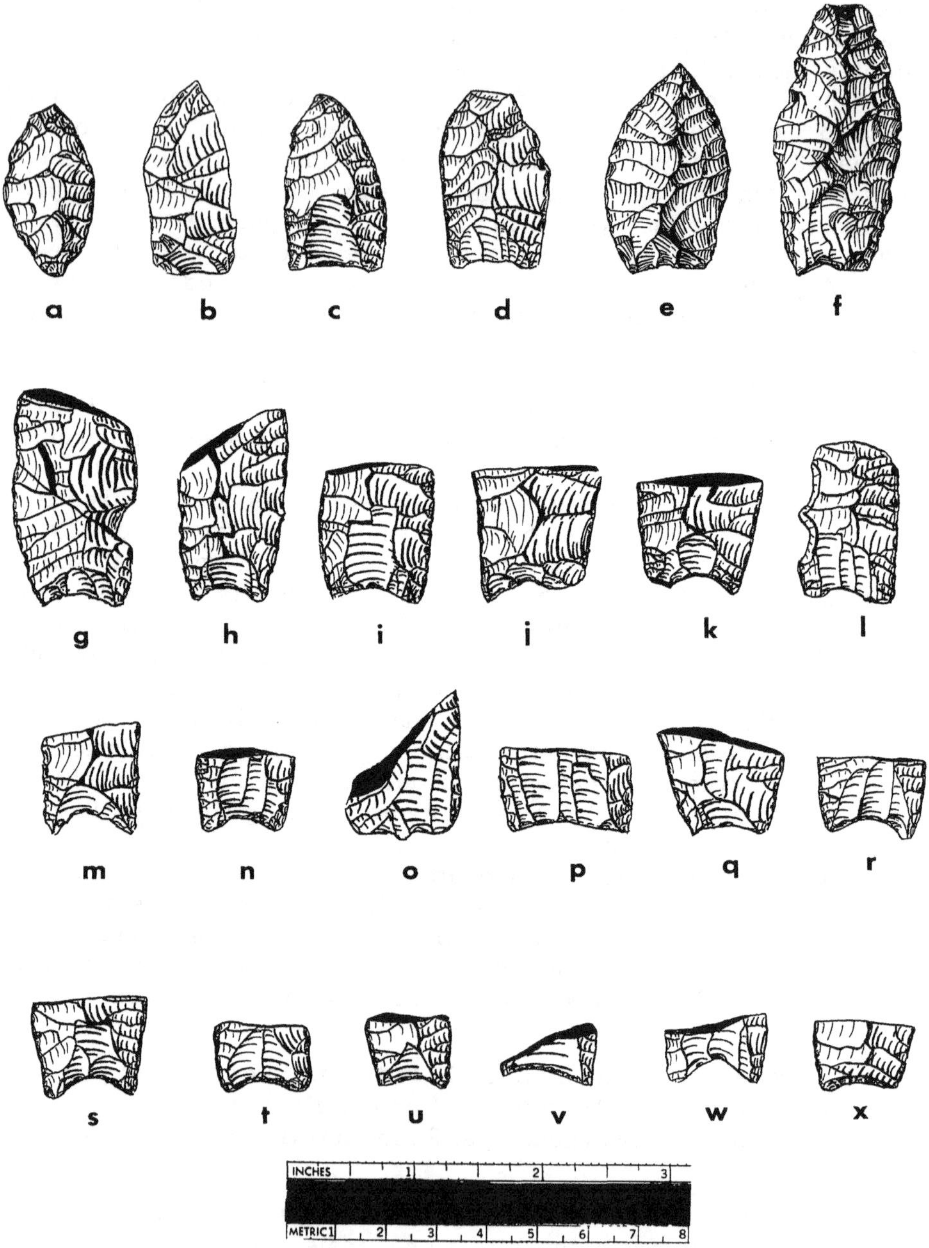


FIG. 6. Artifacts from the Holcombe site. *a-f*, projectile points; *g-h*, projectile point bases.

sample of 44 such objects. In the spring of 1964 Keslin reported 57 points and bases from the site. The increase noted by Keslin was a result of an additional loan collection from DeVisscher obtained in the summers of 1962 and 1963. Late in 1964, I made a detailed examination of all the chippage from the site and found a number of additional bases and bifacial fragments which had been initially included with the general dèbitage from the site. These are included in the present report.

Both the complete points and the bases are analyzed in more detail in the next section of this report. Here we shall only note their major attributes. The unifying characteristics within this series include: fine, parallel pressure flaking; lanceolate outline with a concave base; lateral grinding and a tendency toward basal modification. This basal modification, when present, varies from the removal of a series of long, narrow retouch flakes to full fluting.

The 6 complete points may not be typical of the population represented by the bases. Two of these points are made of white Bayport chert; 1 (Figure 6, *a*, Plate IV, *a*) is double-ended and obviously reworked, the other (Figure 6, *b*, Plate IV, *b*) is crude, eccentric, and has an unusual base. The remaining 4 are made on a light grey Bayport chert. Three of these are rather uniform in length (Figure 6, *c-e*, Plate IV, *c-e*) but 2 have obviously been broken and reworked into shorter points. Only 1 (Figure 6, *f*, Plate IV, *f*) is felt to be typical of the original Holcombe point population (see DeVisscher and Wahla this volume for other complete examples).

The fragments of point bases have the following distribution of chert types: 28 white Bayport chert, 55 light grey Bayport chert, 19 dark grey Bayport chert, 2 exotic cherts. The exotic cherts include 1 black and 1 purple chert.

The point tip fragments (Figure 8, *g*, Plate VI, *g*) represented in the sample are, unquestionably, Paleo-Indian artifacts. They are considerably thinner than the non-Paleo-Indian point series and the majority of them have the typical parallel flaking of the assemblage. Two are made of white Bayport chert, 6 of light grey and 2 of dark grey.

The 19 medial fragments and 21 edge fragments are also a part of the assemblage. The chert distribution within this series includes eight objects of white Bayport chert, 22 objects of light grey Bayport and 10 objects of dark grey Bayport chert.

There are 23 finished bifacial tools (Figure 8, *h-n*, Plate VI, *h-n*) with convergent, but not pointed, tips. I have referred to

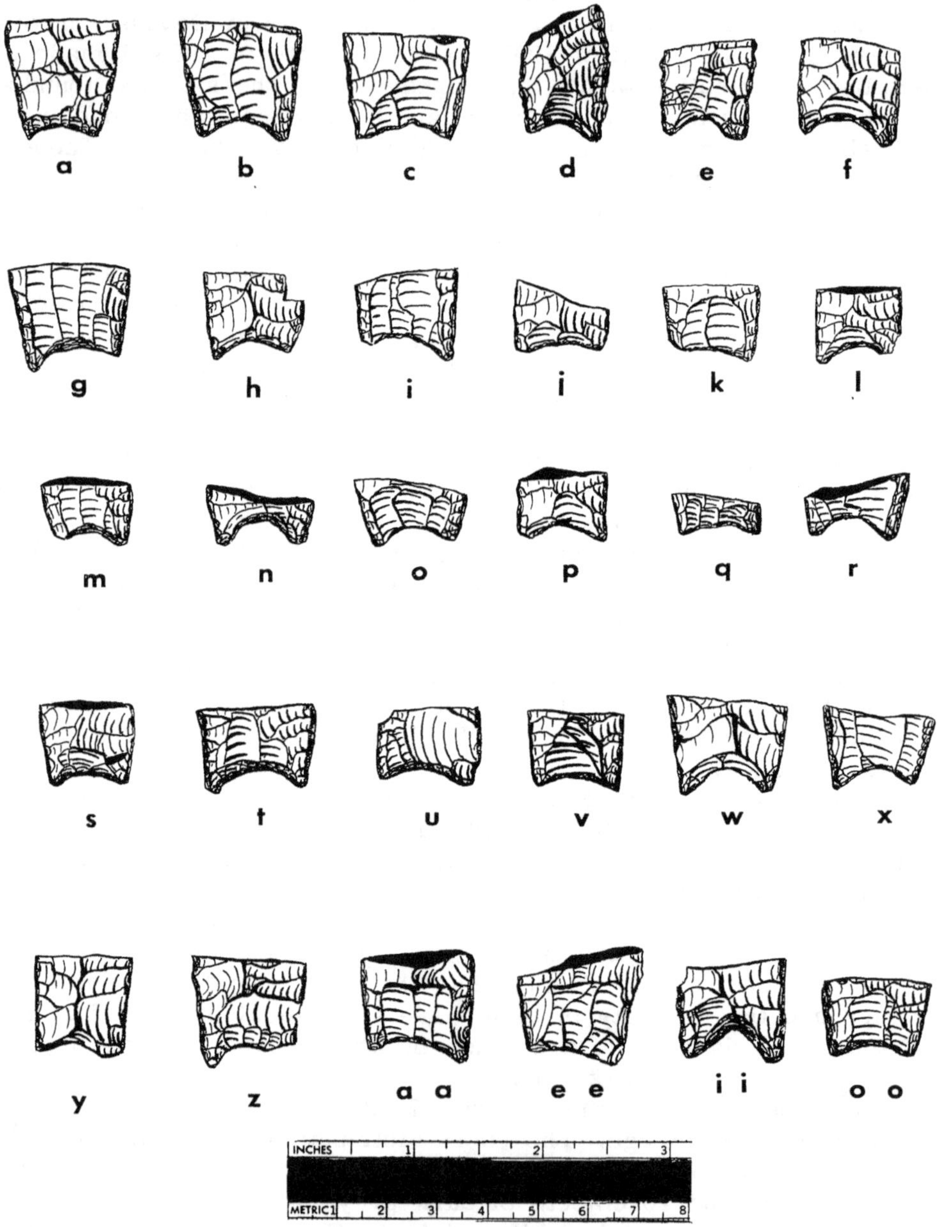


FIG. 7. Artifacts from the Holcombe site. *a-oo*, projectile point bases.

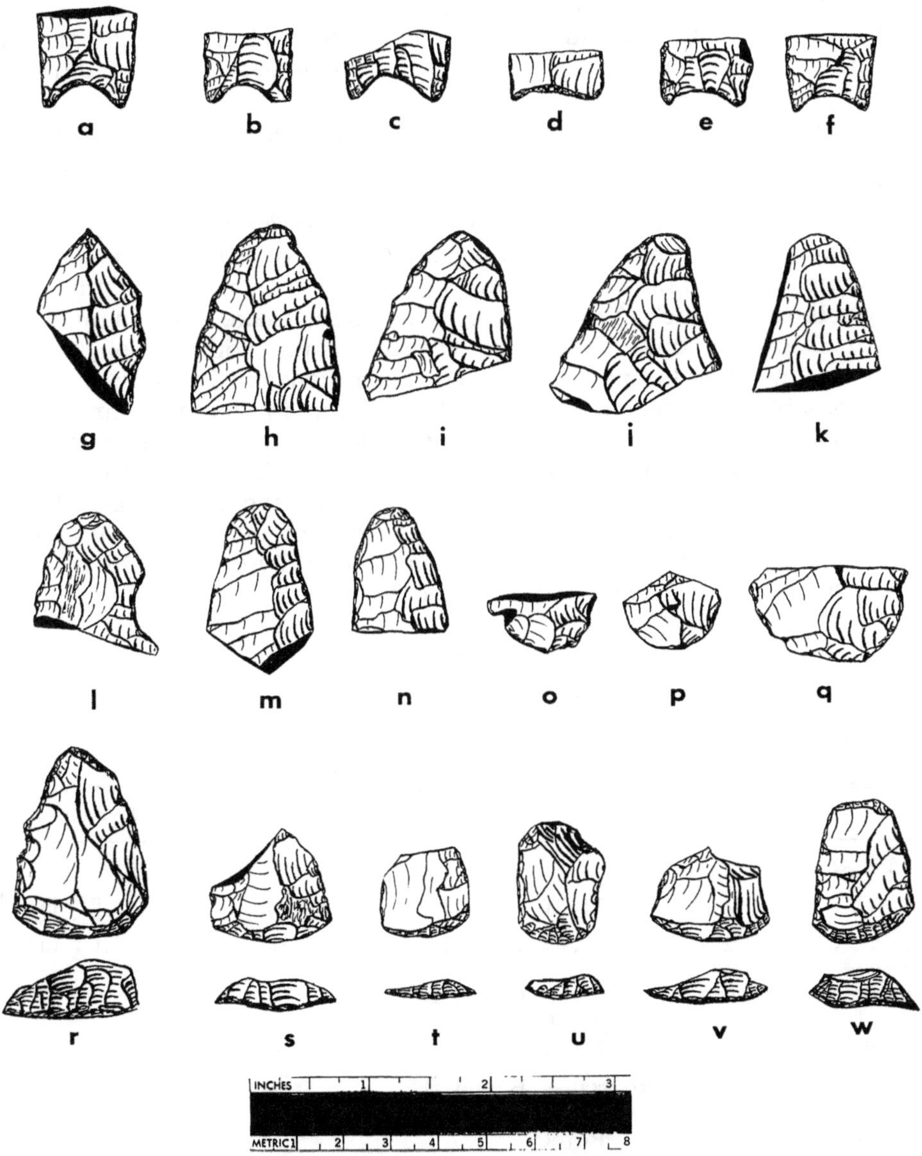


FIG. 8. Artifacts from the Holcombe site. *a-f*, projectile point bases; *g*, pointed tip; *h-n*, convergent tips; *o-q*, rounded tips; *r-w*, end scrapers.

these (Fitting 1964*b*: 232) as thin knives. At present this functional interpretation seems as good as any. This is also true for the 9 fragments of finished bifaces with rounded edges (Figure 8, *o-q*, Plate VI, *o-q*). Out of this series of nonpointed tips there are 12 objects of white Bayport chert, 17 of light grey, and 3 of dark grey.

The mean of the tip and medial fragments of finished bifacial artifacts was 4.70 centimeters with a standard deviation of 1.03 centimeters.

The means and standard deviations of subgroups A, B, and C of Group II gave us a basis for comparison of the thicknesses of preforms and finished artifacts. The t test was used for this comparison (Blalock, 1960: 170-6). We must make an assumption of normalcy for this test. The results of the comparison, however, are so conclusive that we need not concern ourselves with this possible weakness. Our null hypothesis is that the three samples, when paired and compared, represent a single population. The t values are given in Table 23 and it is clear that we must reject our null hypothesis in every instance. We can also note the larger t value for the comparison of subgroups A and C indicating again the intermediate position of Type B preforms between Type A preforms and finished artifacts.

TABLE 23

BIFACE THICKNESS

Results of t Tests Comparing Subgroups of Bifacial Artifacts from the Holcombe Site

| | Subgroup A | Subgroup B | Subgroup C |
|---|---|---|---|
| N. . . . . . . . . . . . . | 13 | 51 | 60 |
| X. . . . . . . . . . . . . | 11.31 cm | 8.06 cm | 4.70 cm |
| S. . . . . . . . . . . . . | 2.02 cm | 1.76 cm | 1.03 cm |

Comparison between Subgroups A and B
t = 5.508 $p < .001$
df = 62 Reject

Comparison between Subgroups B and C
t = 12.000 $p < .001$
df = 109 Reject

Comparison between Subgroups A and C
t = 16.950 $p < .001$
df = 71 Reject

Sub-group D. Six miscellaneous artifacts.

This group is a catchall category for bifacially worked artifacts that do not readily fit into any other group. Three of these are made of chert and three are made of slate.

The first of these objects is a perforator, or scraper, made of a tabular flake of dark grey Bayport chert .3 centimeters in thickness. Each edge has been altered by pressure retouch from one direction but the retouch has been applied from the opposite faces so, technically, it is a bifacial artifact.

There is 1 small bifacially worked object of white Bayport chert which presents us with problems of interpretation. This may be an edge fragment of a finished biface. On the other hand, it may be an extremely crude bifurcate-stemmed point with the tip broken off. If it is a bifurcate-stemmed point, the basal treatment and chert type are very similar to the bifurcate-stemmed points from the Warner School site (Fitting 1964*a*: 93). This object is .3 centimeters thick.

Another unique object is a bifacial denticulate scraper which is made on an exotic light purple and gray-banded chert. It is relatively thick (.7 centimeters) and the concave edges are formed by the removal of several large flakes. A very fine secondary retouch, perhaps the result of usage, is found along several of the concave surfaces.

The other 3 objects are made of slate which has been chipped and battered to make an edge. The largest and most complete of these objects (Plate VII) is made of a greenish slate. It has one pointed end and, as I would reconstruct it, was probably symmetrical. While all edges are battered, none seems to have served as a working edge. The clevage surfaces are dulled only slightly and this could be attributed to weathering. This might indicate that we have a preform rather than a finished artifact. The major portion of this object and 2 smaller fragments came from a single excavation unit. Only 1 fragment came from the plow zone, the other 2 were in place below the plow zone.

The second slate object is purple and is heavily weathered. One edge shows bifacial working and is heavily dulled, perhaps through use. Close examination revealed many small striations along this edge. There are evidences of charring on this object which could have been caused by recent burning of the area.

The third slate object is a purple edge fragment showing the same type of chipping as that of the previous two objects. It appears to have been broken off during the course of bifacial chipping.

### Group III

Group III consists of unifacially worked artifacts made on flakes or, less commonly, blades. There are 62 such artifacts and an additional 5 artifacts which were made on reworked medial and edge fragments of bifacial tools and have their closest analogies in several of the unifacial categories. These tools with counterparts among the unifacial forms are described, but not counted, among the unifacial group. Three subgroups were recognized; a subgroup of standardized scrapers, a subgroup of gravers and a subgroup of retouched flakes and unique items.

> Subgroup A. Standardized scrapers. Eight end scrapers, 6 steep retouch convergent scrapers, 11 fragments steep retouch scrapers, 5 concave scrapers on blades, 4 (8) concave scrapers on flakes (and bifaces).

The 8 end scrapers from the site (Figure 8, *r-w*, Plate VI, *r-w*) show some variation but, in general, conform to the expected pattern. They are marked by a convex working edge, a series of parallel flakes forming a steep retouch and a series of extremely small flakes, ending in hinge fractures, directly on the working edge. With the exception of one fragmentary end scraper the entire series is marked by a slight constriction back of the working edge. In several examples an actual "spur" is present. Three of these scrapers are made on white Bayport chert, 3 on light grey, and 2 on dark grey.

The next was a series of 6 side scrapers with convergent tips (Figure 9, *a-d*, Plate VIII, *a-d*) which are all characterized by a steep retouch, the retouch flakes invariably ending in deep hinge fractures. Four of these scrapers are made on white Bayport chert and 2 on light grey. There are 11 edge fragments which show the same type of steep marginal retouch terminating in deep hinge fractures. They probably belong to side scrapers similar to those with the convergent tips although this can not be positively demonstrated. Three of these are made on white Bayport chert, 5 on light grey, and 2 on dark grey. One is manufactured of exotic chert.

There is a series of concave scrapers manufactured on blades (Figure 9, *e-g*, Plate VIII, *e-g*). Three are complete and 2 are fragmentary, but all have the configuration of blades and a very distinctive pattern of retouch and use. The concave area is prepared by removing a series of small parallel-to-contracting flakes. On one edge of a scraper with two such concavities

(Figure 9, *f*, Plate VIII, *f*) there are signs of further retouch with a series of fine pressure flakes. The other edge of this scraper and the rest of the scrapers are marked by many short flake scars ending in hinge fractures. These flake scars, perhaps, are use marks and would obliterate any fine retouch if such retouch had existed. Four of the scrapers are made of light grey Bayport chert while 1 is made of exotic black chert.

The final series of standardized scrapers consists of 4 concave edge scrapers made on flakes (Figure 9, *k*, Plate VIII, *k*) and 4 made on finished bifacial artifacts which have been broken and reworked (Figure 9, *l-m*, Plate VIII, *l-m*). In this case the concavity seems to have been prepared by removing a single large flake. There is some marginal retouch and an occasional flake has been detached from the reverse face. This, apparently, is caused by use rather than intention. Two of the unifacial forms are made of light grey, and 2 of dark grey Bayport chert. The fact that 2 of the bifacial concave scrapers are double scrapers should also be noted (Figure 9, *l*, Plate VIII, *l*). The intermediate high point between the two concavities does not show the retouch which is characteristic of the gravers from the site.

Subgroup B. Three (4) gravers.

The principle attribute of this category is the presence of a "spur" isolated by secondary retouch flaking (Figure 9, *m-q*, Plate VIII, *m-q*). Two of these gravers are manufactured on flat flakes which are the by-product of bifacial flaking. Both show secondary retouch along several edges in addition to that which contains the graver projection. The third unifacial graver is manufactured on a thick, blocky flake. The graver projection has been isolated by a series of steep parallel flakes similar to those found on end scrapers. In addition, there is some retouch on the projection itself.

There is one graver which has been manufactured on a fragment of a finished bifacial tool (Figure 9, *q*, Plate VIII, *q*). Here the projection is worked from both edges but only on one face. This appears to be a composite tool and there are several small hinge fractures in the concavity along the edge of the tool suggesting that it also functioned as a concave scraper.

Subgroup C. Twenty-Five miscellaneous unifacial artifacts.

The largest group within this series is a catchall category containing retouched and utilized flakes. No standardization was

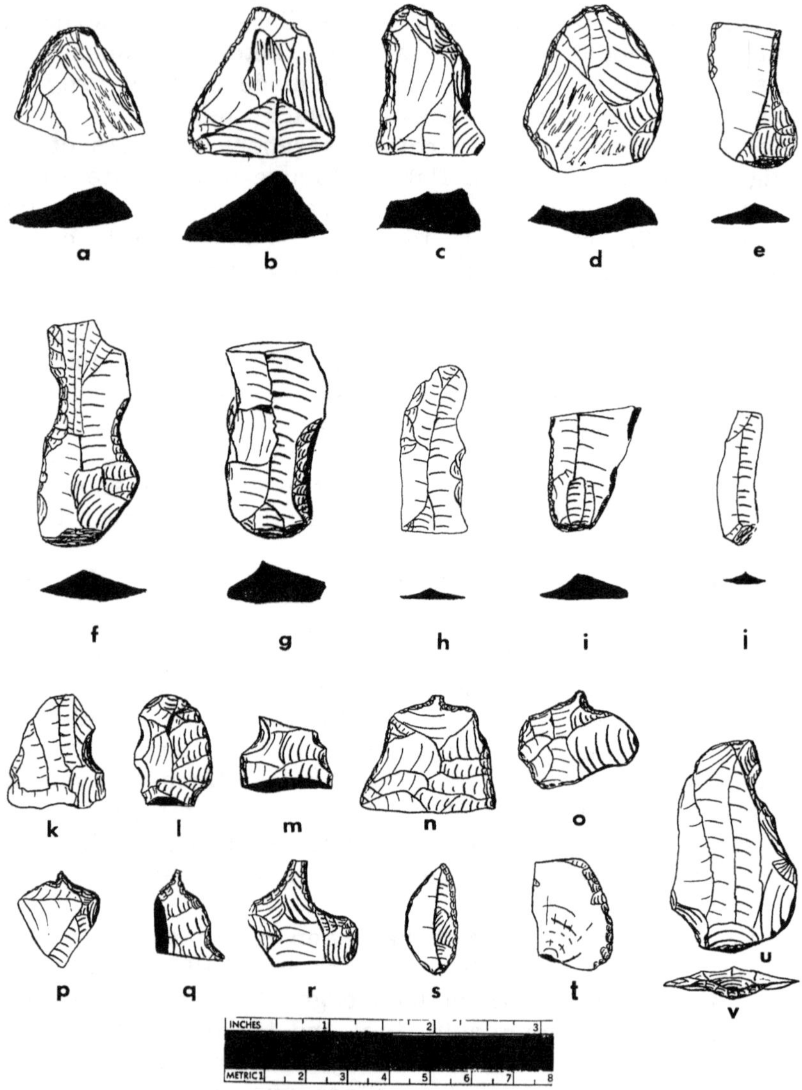


FIG. 9. Artifacts from the Holcome site. *a-d*, steep retouch convergent tip scrapers, *e-g* concave scrapers on blades; *h-i*, retouched blades; *j*, unretouched blade; *k*, concave scraper on a flake; *l-m*, concave scrapers on bifaces, *n-q*, gravers; *r*; drill fragment; *s*, crescent-shaped flake with blunted back; *t*, flake with retouch on bulbar surface; *u*, Levallois flake.

observed in this group. One of these (Figure 9, *t*, Plate VIII, *t*) is interesting because the retouch is found along the bulbar surface of the flake rather than the exterior surface as in all other examples. Another is of interest because, on typological grounds, it would be classed as a Levallois flake (Figure 9, *u-v*, Plate VIII, *u*). Both of these items, however, are unique in the Holcombe sample.

Two retouched and utilized blades (Figure 9, *i*, Plate VIII, *i*) were found at the site. One is a proximal fragment with a remnant of a striking platform and the other is a distal fragment. An additional blade (Figure 9, *j*, Plate VIII, *j*) was recovered from the site but it shows no signs of use or retouch.

One rather unusual scraper was found during the course of the University of Michigan excavations. The working edge of this scraper has been prepared first by the removal of several large flakes and, finally, by a series of fine, resolved flakes. This finishing gives the effect of a gently beveled working edge and sets it apart from the other standardized scrapers.

Another unique object on the site has been interpreted as having been a drill (Figure 9, *r*, Plate VIII, *r*). The "tip" of the object has been broken, but both edges have been worked. There is a tendency for the shaft area to be "rounded off" by the removal of several flakes, ending in hinge fractures, which have been removed from the interior surface of the flake. The width measurement of the shaft along the interior surface is, therefore, somewhat less than the maximum shaft measurement.

The last artifact from the site is a small, crescent-shaped flake (Figure 9, *s*, Plate VIII, *s*) with a steep backing, perhaps even blunting, along the rounded edge, and a series of retouch flakes along the straighter of the two edges. The retouch pattern gives the effect of a sharpened short edge and a blunt rounded edge.

Out of the last series of 25 unifacial objects there were 9 artifacts of white Bayport chert, 13 artifacts of light grey Bayport chert, 1 of dark grey and 2 artifacts of exotic materials. The distribution of chert and tool types is given in Table 24.

## Projectile Point Bases

In a preliminary report of a statistical analysis of a rather limited part of the sample of points and bases from the Holcombe site, I had found some indications of possible projectile point groupings (Fitting, 1964*b*). While the over-all sample was rather

TABLE 24

PALEO-INDIAN ARTIFACTS FROM THE HOLCOMBE SITE

Artifacts Listed by Group, Subgroup, and Category with the Frequencies of the Chert Types and Totals of these Categories at the Site

| | White Bayport | Light Grey Bayport | Dark Grey Bayport | Exotic | Total |
|---|---|---|---|---|---|
| Group I . . . . . . . . . . | 4 | . . . | 1 | . . . | 5 |
| Group II | | | | | |
| Subgroup A . . . . . . . | 13 | . . . | . . . | . . . | 13 |
| Subgroup B | | | | | |
| Complete . . . . . . . | 2 | 2 | . . . | 1 | 5 |
| End fragments . . . . | 17 | 11 | 8 | . . . | 36 |
| Medial fragments . . | 3 | 4 | 3 | . . . | 10 |
| Edge fragments . . . | 9 | 14 | 32 | 1 | 56 |
| Subgroup C | | | | | |
| Points . . . . . . . . . | 2 | 4 | . . . | . . . | 6 |
| Bases . . . . . . . . . | 28 | 55 | 19 | 2 | 104 |
| Point tips . . . . . . . | 2 | 6 | 2 | . . . | 10 |
| Edge and medial fragments . . . . . . | 8 | 22 | 10 | . . . | 40 |
| Convergent and rounded tips . . . . | 12 | 17 | 3 | . . . | 32 |
| Subgroup D . . . . . . . . | 1 | . . . | 1 | 4 | 6 |
| Group III | | | | | |
| Subgroup A | | | | | |
| End scrapers. . . . . | 3 | 3 | 2 | . . . | 8 |
| Convergent scrapers | 4 | 2 | . . . | . . . | 6 |
| Scraper fragments . | 3 | 5 | 2 | 1 | 11 |
| Concave scrapers on blades . . . . . . | . . . | 4 | . . . | 1 | 5 |
| Concave scrapers on flakes. . . . . . . | . . . | 2 | 2 | . . . | 4 |
| Subgroup B . . . . . . . | . . . | 3 | . . . | . . . | 3 |
| Subgroup C . . . . . . . | 9 | 13 | 1 | 2 | 25 |
| Totals . . . . . . . . | 120 | 167 | 86 | 12 | 385 |
| Percentages . . . . . . . | 31.17 | 43.38 | 22.33 | 3.12 | |

homogeneous, an association between basal treatment and basal width was suggested. Further statistical comparisons within the larger sample seemed in order so a variety of tests were undertaken during the present study.

I restudied the entire series of points and bases from the site and recorded information on them in a slightly different manner from that in the first study. While the metric attributes, basal width, and thickness remain the same, I made some alteration in the categories of chert and basal alteration. The chert categories are those described earlier in this report. The changes in categories of basal alteration, thinning, and fluting, have come about through discussions and correspondence with Arthur Jelinek, Olaf Prufer, William Roosa, and Richard Keslin. Keslin, in his 1964 Michigan Academy Paper, criticized the categories which I had used in my 1962 study (published in 1964). The more rigid categories used in the present study may prove to be more satisfactory.

Seven attributes were recorded for the present study (Table 25). Four of these were used in the earlier study—basal width, basal thickness, method of basal alteration, and chert type. Three additional attributes were those of provenience: excavation unit, area on the site, and level. Only the latter two were used in the statistical examination.

Basal width and basal thickness were measured at the extreme of the basal concavity. The total width at this point, which could also be interpreted as the hafting width, was measured.

The chert categories have been described before. They consisted of white, light grey, and dark grey Bayport chert. Only two of the bases were made of exotic materials so this category was too small to include in the tests involving chert groups.

Five categories of basal alteration were used in this study. As Keslin mentioned, most of the bases which I had classed as unaltered were "nibbled" and some even had a thin crescent-shaped flake removed from the basal area. A certain amount of basal alteration would be expected as a part of general bifacial working. In the earlier study I had divided the points and bases into altered and unaltered groups on the basis of what I thought was intentional or unintentional alteration.

In the present study unaltered bases are marked by the absence of any alteration beyond a crushing which could be construed as a preparation of the striking platform at the base. All removal of thin flakes, whether they are the typical thin, parallel flakes, the rarer short expanding flakes or even rarer flutes, was classified as modification. Therefore, I found only five bases in the sample of 110 which I would class as unmodified on both faces. In the earlier report I classified 11 out of 44 bases as unmodified on both faces.

I also made a distinction between the removal of multiple, short flakes from the base, or basal thinning, and the removal of one or several long flakes from the base, or actual fluting. This allowed the establishment of six categories, only five of which were found at the site. A base could be (1) unmodified on both faces; (2) unmodified on one face and thinned on the second; (3) unmodified on one face and fluted on the second face; (4) thinned on both faces; or (5) thinned on one face and fluted on the second. The sixth possible category, fluted on both faces, was not represented.

The individual provenience units were recorded but they provided too small a sample for statistical comparison. Instead, the areas of the site, defined in Chapter II, were used for comparison. Three levels were also used in this analysis. Level one represents material found by the University of Michigan on the surface of excavation units or in the plow zone of these units. Level two consists of the area between the base of the plow zone and .3 feet below the base of the plow zone. Level three consists of all material found below this depth.

The information which was recorded on these points and bases is presented in Table 25.

The statistical tests which were run on the sample were of two types. The first series consisted of analysis of variance run on metric attributes between different categories of nonmetric attributes. The analysis was done with the 7090 computer of the University of Michigan using a program prepared by Charles Eyman of the University of Michigan Museum of Anthropology. Eyman had prepared this program for the analysis of skeletal data but it proved readily adaptable to an analysis of point bases.

The second series were tests for attribute association such as I had used in the earlier study and as described by Spaulding (1960). These were greatly simplified by the use of IBM cards and a card sorter which replaced the MacBee keysort cards previously used (Fitting, 1965*a*, 1965*b*).

Since Eyman's original program was designed for a maximum of four categories and we had five categories of basal treatment, some reorganization was necessary. The result was an analysis of variance on two metric attributes for five, rather than three, nonmetric categories. The groupings are given in Table 26 along with the sample size, total sum, sum of squares, sum of the values squared divided by the sample size, the degrees of freedom and the F values.

None of the F values are significant for the requisite degrees

TABLE 25

POINT BASE ATTRIBUTES

Metric and Nonmetric Attributes to Projectile Point Bases from the Holcombe Site (Measurements in millimeters).

| Catalog Number | Specimen Number | Basal Width | Basal Thickness | Basal Treatment | Chert | Grinding | Area | Unit | Level |
|---|---|---|---|---|---|---|---|---|---|
| 57881 . . . | 1 | . . | 2 | . . | 1 | + | 3 | 100-140 | 1 |
| 57911 . . . | 2 | 17 | 3 | 2 | 2 | + | 2 | 570-540 | 1 |
| 57918 . . . | 3 | 23 | 4 | 4 | 4 | + | 2 | 570-550 | 1 |
| 57921 . . . | 4 | 21 | 3 | 3 | 2 | + | 2 | 580-540 | 1 |
| 57921 . . . | 5 | . . | 3 | 4 | 2 | + | 2 | 580-540 | 1 |
| 57921 . . . | 6 | . . | 2 | 3 | 2 | + | 2 | 580-540 | 1 |
| 57921 . . . | 7 | . . | 2 | . . | 2 | + | 2 | 580-540 | 1 |
| 57921 . . . | 8 | . . | . . | . . | 2 | + | 2 | 580-540 | 1 |
| 57921 . . . | 9 | . . | . . | . . | 2 | . . | 2 | 580-540 | 1 |
| 57923 . . . | 10 | 19 | 3 | 4 | 2 | + | 2 | 590-540 | 1 |
| 57924 . . . | 11 | 20 | 3 | 3 | 2 | + | 2 | 590-540 | 1 |
| 57924 . . . | 12 | . . | 3 | 4 | 3 | + | 2 | 590-540 | 1 |
| 57943 . . . | 13 | 18 | 3 | 5 | 1 | + | 1 | 610-490 | 2 |
| 57947 . . . | 14 | 19 | 3 | 2 | 2 | + | 1 | 610-500 | 1 |
| 57947 . . . | 15 | 20 | 3 | 4 | 2 | + | 1 | 610-500 | 1 |
| 57947 . . . | 16 | . . | 3 | . . | 3 | . . | 1 | 610-500 | 1 |
| 57962 . . . | 17 | . . | 3 | 4 | 3 | + | 1 | 620-470 | 1 |
| 57975 . . . | 18 | 14 | 3 | 3 | 2 | + | 1 | 620-480 | 2 |
| 57977 . . . | 19 | 17 | 3 | 3 | 1 | + | 1 | 610-490 | 3 |
| 57982 . . . | 20 | . . | 2 | 4 | 3 | + | 1 | 620-480 | 1 |
| 57983 . . . | 21 | 20 | 3 | 3 | 1 | + | 1 | 620-480 | 3 |
| 57993 . . . | 22 | 20 | 3 | 3 | 3 | + | 1 | 610-490 | 2 |
| 57997 . . . | 23 | 18 | 2 | 4 | 2 | + | 1 | 620-490 | 2 |
| 58007 . . . | 24 | . . | . . | . . | 1 | + | 1 | 620-490 | 3 |
| 58010 . . . | 25 | 17 | 3 | 3 | 2 | + | 1 | 620-490 | 3 |
| 58011 . . . | 26 | 18 | 3 | 2 | 1 | + | 1 | 620-490 | 3 |
| 58017 . . . | 27 | 17 | 3 | 3 | 2 | + | 1 | 620-490 | 2 |
| 58019 . . . | 28 | . . | 4 | 3 | 2 | + | 1 | 620-500 | 1 |

TABLE 25 (continued)

| Catalog Number | Specimen Number | Basal Width | Basal Thickness | Basal Treatment | Chert | Grinding | Area | Unit | Level |
|---|---|---|---|---|---|---|---|---|---|
| 58023 . . . | 29 | 20 | 3 | 3 | 2 | + | 1 | 620-500 | 2 |
| 58025 . . . | 30 | 20 | 3 | 1 | 2 | + | 1 | 620-500 | 2 |
| 58026 . . . | 31 | 20 | 3 | 4 | 2 | + | 1 | 620-500 | 2 |
| 58052 . . . | 32 | . . | 3 | 4 | 3 | + | 1 | 620-500 | 3 |
| 58056 . . . | 33 | 19 | 2 | 4 | 1 | + | 1 | 620-500 | 2 |
| 58058 . . . | 34 | 17 | 3 | 4 | 1 | + | 1 | 620-510 | 1 |
| 58058 . . . | 35 | 19 | 3 | 3 | 3 | + | 1 | 620-510 | 1 |
| 58066 . . . | 36 | . . | . . | 3 | 1 | + | 1 | 640-490 | 1 |
| 58069 . . . | 37 | . . | 3 | 4 | 3 | + | 1 | 630-480 | 1 |
| 58079 . . . | 38 | . . | . . | . . | 1 | + | 1 | 630-480 | 3 |
| 58083 . . . | 39 | . . | 2 | 4 | 2 | + | 1 | 630-490 | 1 |
| 58084 . . . | 40 | 16 | 4 | 3 | 1 | - | 1 | 630-490 | 2 |
| 58113 . . . | 41 | . . | 3 | 4 | 1 | + | 1 | 630-500 | 1 |
| 58118 . . . | 42 | . . | 3 | . . | 1 | + | 1 | 630-500 | 2 |
| 58128 . . . | 43 | 22 | 4 | 2 | 2 | + | 1 | 630-510 | 1 |
| 58135 . . . | 44 | 20 | 2 | 3 | 2 | + | 1 | 610-490 | 1 |
| 58135 . . . | 45 | 18 | 3 | 1 | 3 | + | 1 | 610-490 | 1 |
| 58137 . . . | 46 | 17 | 2 | 3 | 2 | + | 1 | 620-470 | 1 |
| 58139 . . . | 47 | 16 | 3 | 3 | 1 | + | 1 | 620-480 | 1 |
| 58139 . . . | 48 | 17 | 3 | 1 | 2 | + | 1 | 620-480 | 1 |
| 58140 . . . | 49 | 18 | 3 | 3 | 2 | + | 1 | 620-480 | 1 |
| 58140 . . . | 50 | 18 | 3 | 2 | 2 | + | 1 | 620-480 | 1 |
| 58142 . . . | 51 | 20 | 3 | 3 | 2 | + | 1 | 620-490 | 1 |
| 58142 . . . | 52 | . . | 3 | 3 | 2 | + | 1 | 620-490 | 1 |
| D36-3 . . . | 53 | 21 | 2 | 4 | 1 | + | . . | . . . | . . |
| D36-4 . . . | 54 | 19 | 2 | 4 | 1 | + | . . | . . . | . . |
| D36-6 . . . | 55 | 18 | 3 | 4 | 2 | . . | . . | . . . | . . |
| D36-12 . . | 56 | . . | 3 | . . | 1 | . . | . . | . . . | . . |

TABLE 25 (continued)

| Catalog Number | Specimen Number | Basal Width | Basal Thickness | Basal Treatment | Chert | Grinding | Area | Unit | Level |
|---|---|---|---|---|---|---|---|---|---|
| D36-24 . . | 57 | . . | 4 | . . | 2 | + | . . | . . . | . . |
| D36-30 . . | 58 | 18 | 3 | 3 | 2 | + | . . | . . . | . . |
| D36-37 . . | 59 | 16 | 3 | 5 | 3 | + | . . | . . . | . . |
| D36-38 . . | 60 | 22 | 4 | 4 | 2 | + | . . | . . . | . . |
| D36-39 . . | 61 | 17 | 2 | 5 | 2 | + | . . | . . . | . . |
| D36-40 . . | 62 | 17 | 3 | 1 | 2 | + | . . | . . . | . . |
| D36-41 . . | 63 | 20 | 2 | 3 | 2 | + | . . | . . . | . . . |
| D36-43 . . | 64 | 20 | 2 | 3 | 2 | + | . . | . . . | . . |
| D36-44 . . | 65 | 20 | 3 | 4 | 2 | + | . . | . . . | . . |
| D36-45 . . | 66 | 20 | 3 | 4 | 2 | + | . . | . . . | . . |
| D36-46 . . | 67 | 21 | 3 | 4 | 1 | + | . . | . . . | . . |
| D36-47 . . | 68 | 16 | 3 | 4 | 2 | + | . . | . . . | . . |
| D36-48 . . | 69 | 17 | 3 | 2 | 2 | + | . . | . . . | . . |
| D36-52 . . | 70 | . . | 3 | . . | 2 | + | . . | . . . | . . . |
| D36-78 . . | 71 | 27 | 8 | . . | 2 | - | . . | . . . | . . |
| D36-114 . | 72 | 19 | 3 | 5 | 2 | + | . . | . . . | . . |
| D36-115 . | 73 | 20 | 3 | 5 | 1 | + | . . | . . . | . . |
| D36-117 . | 74 | 21 | 2 | 3 | 3 | + | . . | . . . | . . |
| D36-118 . | 75 | 16 | 3 | 2 | 2 | + | . . | . . . | . . |
| D36-123 . | 76 | 17 | 2 | 4 | 1 | + | . . | . . . | . . |
| D36-124 . | 77 | 21 | 3 | 3 | 1 | + | . . | . . . | . . |
| D36-125 . | 78 | 19 | 2 | 5 | 1 | + | . . | . . . | . . |
| D36-126 . | 79 | 25 | 3 | 5 | 2 | + | . . | . . . | . . |
| D36-128 . | 80 | 19 | 3 | 3 | 1 | + | . . | . . . | . . |
| D36-129 . | 81 | 18 | 2 | 5 | 1 | + | . . | . . . | . . |
| D36-130 . | 82 | 20 | 3 | 5 | 2 | - | . . | . . . | . . |
| D36-131 . | 83 | 20 | 3 | 4 | 2 | + | . . | . . . | . . |
| D36-132 . | 34 | 18 | 2 | 3 | 3 | + | . . | . . . | . . |
| D36-133 . | 85 | 18 | 3 | 3 | 1 | + | . . | . . . | . . |

TABLE 25 (continued)

| Catalog Number | Specimen Number | Basal Width | Basal Thickness | Basal Treatment | Chert | Grinding | Area | Unit | Level |
|---|---|---|---|---|---|---|---|---|---|
| D36-156 . | 86 | 18 | 3 | 4 | 1 | + | . . | . . . | . . |
| D36-157 . | 87 | 18 | 3 | 4 | 3 | + | . . | . . . | . . |
| D36-159 . | 88 | 22 | 3 | 2 | 2 | + | . . | . . . | . . |
| D36-164 . | 89 | 70 | 3 | 4 | 2 | + | . . | . . . | . . |
| D36-165 . | 90 | 16 | 2 | 4 | 2 | + | . . | . . . | . . |
| D36-166 . | 91 | 18 | 3 | 4 | 2 | + | . . | . . . | . . |
| D36 . . . . | 92 | 17 | 3 | 2 | 1 | + | . . | . . . | . . |
| D36 . . . . | 93 | . . | 5 | 5 | 3 | . . | . . | . . . | . . |
| D36 . . . . | 94 | 22 | 3 | 4 | 2 | + | . . | . . . | . . |
| D36 . . . . | 95 | 19 | 3 | 2 | 3 | + | . . | . . . | . . |
| D36 . . . . | 96 | 18 | 3 | 4 | 4 | + | . . | . . . | . . |
| D36 . . . . | 97 | . . | 3 | 4 | 2 | + | . . | . . . | . . |
| D36 . . . . | 98 | 17 | 2 | 4 | 2 | + | . . | . . . | . . |
| D36 . . . . | 99 | 18 | 3 | 5 | 2 | + | . . | . . . | . . |
| D36 . . . . | 100 | 18 | 3 | 3 | 3 | + | . . | . . . | . . |
| D36 . . . . | 101 | . . | 3 | 4 | 3 | + | . . | . . . | . . |
| D36 . . . . | 102 | . . | 4 | 1 | 1 | + | . . | . . . | . . |
| D36 . . . . | 103 | . . | 3 | 3 | 1 | + | . . | . . . | . . |
| D36 . . . . | 104 | . . | 3 | 4 | 3 | + | . . | . . . | . . |
| D36 . . . . | 105 | 19 | 3 | 3 | 2 | - | . . | . . . | . . |
| D36 . . . . | 106 | 20 | 2 | 3 | 2 | + | . . | . . . | . . |
| D37 . . . . | 107 | 17 | 3 | 4 | 2 | + | . . | . . . | . . |
| D36 . . . . | 108 | 18 | 2 | 4 | 2 | + | . . | . . . | . . |
| *120-100. | 109 | 18 | 2 | 3 | 3 | + | 3 | 120-100 | . . |
| *120-100. | 110 | 19 | 2 | 3 | 1 | + | 3 | 120-100 | . . |

*Unit number penciled on artifact.

TABLE 26

RESULTS OF ANALYSIS VARIANCE

The Results of the Analysis of Variance on Metric Attributes for Level, Chert Type and the Five Types of Basal Treatment*

| †Comparison | N | x | $(x^2)$ | ‡$\frac{(x)^2}{N}$ | df | F |
|---|---|---|---|---|---|---|
| Level | 32 | 595 | 11173 | 11065 | 2,29 | .22 |
| Chert | 79 | 1486 | 28276 | 27953 | 2,76 | .13 |
| Width | | | | | | |
| Basal groups 1, 2, 3, and 4 | 70 | 1310 | 24736 | 24517 | 3,66 | .23 |
| Basal groups 1 and 5 | 14 | 262 | 4966 | 4906 | 1,12 | .57 |
| Basal groups 2, 3, 4, and 5 | 76 | 1428 | 27098 | 26834 | 3,72 | .22 |
| Level | 47 | 136 | 406 | 394 | 2,44 | .11 |
| Thickness | | | | | | |
| Chert | 103 | 297 | 915 | 856 | 2,100 | .00 |
| Basal groups 1, 2, 3, and 4 | 86 | 244 | 716 | 694 | 3,82 | 1.97 |
| Basal groups 1 and 5 | 16 | 48 | 152 | 144 | 1,14 | .53 |
| Basal groups 2, 3, 4 and 5 | 92 | 260 | 764 | 753 | 3,88 | .01 |

*No tests were run between areas since so few bases were found outside of Area I.

†For more convenient computer handling the measurements for the series of tests were recorded in millimeters instead of centimeters.

‡This value has been rounded off to the nearest whole number for this problem. The fourth decimal place was used in the test.

of freedom. The results of this analysis indicate that there is no association between the metric and nonmetric attributes.

The results of the tests which were run for attribute association are given in Table 27. Several of the possible combinations had to be excluded because of insufficient sample size. There seemed to be no point in testing such attributes as area and level for association with each other so this too was excluded.

Out of the thirteen tests which were run, the observed and expected distributions were found to be identical in three

TABLE 27

ASSOCIATION OF ATTRIBUTES

Results of Chi-square Test for Observed and Expected Combinations of Attributes if Chance Alone were Affecting the Distribution

| Comparison | N | df | $x^2$ | p < |
|---|---|---|---|---|
| Base/chert . . . . . . . . . . . . . . . . | 74 | 2 | 3.78 | .20 |
| Base/area. . . . . . . . . . . . . . . . . | 43 | 2 | 2.53 | .30 |
| Base/level . . . . . . . . . . . . . . . . | 41 | 2 | .00 | [p>.99] |
| Base/thickness . . . . . . . . . . . . . | 92 | 2 | .24 | .99 |
| Base/width . . . . . . . . . . . . . . . . | 79 | 1 | .82 | .50 |
| Chert/area . . . . . . . . . . . . . . . . | 50 | 2 | 4.81 | .10 |
| Chert/level . . . . . . . . . . . . . . . . | 51 | 4 | 10.03 | .05 |
| Chert/thickness . . . . . . . . . . . . . | 103 | 2 | 1.10 | .90 |
| Chert/width. . . . . . . . . . . . . . . . | 83 | 1 | .27 | .70 |
| Area/thickness . . . . . . . . . . . . . | 49 | 2 | 6.63 | .05 |
| Level/thickness . . . . . . . . . . . . . | 42 | 2 | .00 | [p>.99] |
| Level/width. . . . . . . . . . . . . . . . | 27 | 1 | .00 | [p>.99] |
| Thickness/width. . . . . . . . . . . . . | 79 | 2 | 4.56 | .30 |

instances. In eight instances the difference between the observed and expected distributions was not significant. In only two instances, the associations between area and basal thickness and between level and chert type, did we find significant differences between observed and expected distributions.

When we examined the first of these associations we found that the high value for chi-square was caused by discrepancies in Area III. Only three bases were recovered from Area III so the sample size was not really valid to make this type of test. The fact that all three bases were only .2 of a centimeter thick may have some distributional significance but I can see no typological significance.

In the test for association between chert type and level the discrepancy was caused primarily by a greater than expected number of white Bayport bases in level three; five were found while only two were expected by chance association. While this may be significant for distribution studies, and the study of the dèbitage indicated that it is not, it too has no typological significance.

The results of this quantitative examination show an even greater uniformity than that which I had suggested in my earlier study. With a much larger sample and more refined methods of classification and analysis the possible associations suggested in my earlier study did not prove valid.

## Manufacturing Methods

With the above information in mind it is possible to reconstruct the process of artifact manufacture at the Holcombe site. The raw material was obtained in the form of small nodules from a source some distance from the site. These nodules were probably no larger than 6 inches in diameter with the majority of them being much smaller than this.

At some point, probably immediately after obtaining the raw material, the nodules were worked into rough bifacial preforms. These preforms were transported to the site where they were finished into tools.

The sample of Type A preforms from the site, the extremely rough preforms manufactured from the nodule, is probably not typical of the entire Type A preform population. They are shorter than even the Type B preforms and are made of the poorest white Bayport chert. They may represent preforms discarded at this stage of manufacture. The better quality preforms were either finished into artifacts or carried on to the next camp. It is doubtful that a group with the apparent mobility of the Holcombe peoples would be able to transport too many preforms at any one time.

The next stage in manufacture can be deduced from both the artifacts and the dèbitage. Apparently the edges of Type A preforms were ground to prepare a striking platform. This has been suggested as one means of preparing a point base for fluting at this cultural horizon in the New World (Prufer, 1962*b*: 5, 8; Roosa, 1963: 45). The consensus of the Les Eyzies conference (Jelinek: personal communication) is that this was done to give the hammer a better "bite" in using the soft-hammer technique. The flakes of bifacial retouch were struck from the Type A preforms during this stage of manufacture.

The next stage in the manufacture of a bifacial artifact was the Type B preform. These preforms were prepared by percussion and, in their final stage, lacked edge grinding which may have been caused by the fact that most of the further finishing was done by pressure flaking where grinding would not be helpful.

It is at this stage in manufacture that we have the interesting technique of preparing preforms by the application of heat. In our examination of dèbitage we noted an association between block fracture flakes, dark grey Bayport chert and fired areas. We also noted a large number of block fracture edge fragments among our Type B preforms. An examination of Table 24 will also show a higher percentage of dark grey Bayport chert among Type B preforms and finished bifacial artifacts than among all other classes of artifacts.

One of the things brought out by the Les Eyzies conference (Jelinek: personal communication) is that there are many instances of artifacts being treated with heat before they are finished by pressure retouch. From experimentation Donald Crabtree was able to demonstrate that a fusion of silicates takes place at a temperature of 400 to 500 degrees Fahrenheit which makes flint working easier. The spalling and "heat pops" usually associated with heat application occur at higher temperatures. Crabtree found that many of the "ribbon flaking" traditions utilized this heat alteration technique. The finished bifacial artifacts from the Holcombe site are all characterized by the removal of long, thin, parallel flakes.

The evidence from the Holcombe site seems to indicate that Type B preforms were placed in the sand near a fire area and heated before they were finished into bifacial tools. The control of heat under these circumstances would have been difficult and many artifacts were apparently broken at this stage of manufacture. As an aside, it might be mentioned that Crabtree found the most effective method of heat preparation was to bury the preforms in sand while they were being heated. This would be an experimental duplication of the natural conditions present at the Holcombe site.

The Type B preforms, after heat preparation, were finished into thin bifacial tools of several types. From relative frequencies of artifact types it would appear that most of these were made into projectile points. In addition to projectile points there were thin bifacial objects with rounded or convergent tips which apparently served as knives. It is unfortunate that we have no complete Holcombe knives but then we have only one complete point which is not a discard or has not been reworked. The Holcombe knappers were very careful of their finished artifacts which we might expect in light of the difficulty of obtaining raw material. The frequency of broken artifacts, however, probably reflects the preparation of artifacts at the site since broken forms would have to be replaced.

The fragments of slate bifaces present a problem. They have no obvious function. It is possible that they were used in the treatment of hides. They may have analogies in the large bifaces from the Brohm site (MacNeish, 1952: 34) and the Hi-Lo site (Fitting, 1963*b*: 92). There is no evidence that they were ceremonial objects.

The unifacial objects were manufactured primarily on flakes with a small occurrence of blades. Blades do not form a large part of the assemblage at Holcombe, probably because of the small size of Bayport chert nodules. Blades seemed to be used primarily for a specific tool type, a concave or spokeshape scraper. I would tend to think of this as a woodworking tool, perhaps used in the preparation of shafts. The concave scrapers on flakes may also have served this purpose.

The steep retouch scrapers, convergent tip steep retouch scrapers, and end scrapers seem to reflect the working of hides. In comparison to other Paleo-Indian sites the low frequency of end scrapers is striking. One explanation for this is that the part of the butchering process utilizing end scrapers was carried out at the kill site rather than in the camp site. Another possible explanation is that end scrapers are less likely to break than larger flake scrapers and bifacial tools. It is evident that these people did not throw away anything if it could possibly be reused. There are many small curved retouch flakes which might be dèbris from retouching end scrapers. I believe that the Holcombe people carried most of their end scrapers along with them and that they were resharpened when they became dull rather than discarded.

One tool type which one might expect to find at a site such as Holcombe was absent. Since burins have been reported from a number of sites in the New World (Epstein, 1960, 1963) we made a detailed examination of the chippage to see if they might be present at Holcombe. Many of the block fracture flakes and heat-fractured preforms had the general appearance of burins. Examination under a microscope, however, revealed no percussion marks. The majority of the sample of block fracture flakes was also examined by both Jelinek and Anta White. We found nothing in the sample that positively resembled an Old World burin. This does not preclude the possibility that burins may be found on other Paleo-Indian sites in Michigan.

IV

# DISTRIBUTION OF CULTURE MATERIAL AT THE HOLCOMBE SITE

## Vertical Distribution

The only natural stratigraphic break within the levels containing cultural material at the Holcombe site was between the plow zone and the area under the plow zone. An arbitrary division was made within the area undisturbed by the plow. For comparative purposes this gave us three levels: Level one, the plow zone; level two, the area directly below the plow zone to a depth of .3 feet below the plow zone; level three, the level below .3 feet below the plow zone which still contained cultural material.

The number of flakes of bifacial retouch and block fracture flakes in the three levels are compared in Table 28. The expected chance distribution was calculated and the observed and expected values tested by chi-square. The value of chi-square was rather high and the difference was significant, although the relationship was not strong. The difference was caused by greater than expected numbers of block fracture flakes in level one and greater than expected numbers of flakes of bifacial retouch, particularly those without striking platforms, in the deepest level. I do not believe this has any cultural significance. If we recall the average weight of these flakes (Table 8, p. 27) we can note that the larger flakes (block fracture flakes) are found more frequently in the higher levels while lighter flakes (flakes of bifacial retouch without striking platforms) are found in the lower levels.

The same type of test was made on small retouch flakes and all other flakes from the three levels at the site (Table 29). Here there was a highly significant, but relatively weak, difference. This difference was caused by the occurrence of more than the expected number of larger flakes in the upper levels and many more than the expected number of small retouch flakes in the lowest level.

What we seem to be dealing with here is a tendency for the smaller flakes to settle or be trampled more easily into the loose sand of the site. Where the difference in flake size is slight, as

TABLE 28

FLAKES AND LEVELS

Observed and Expected Numbers of Flakes of Bifacial Retouch and Block Fracture Flakes Found in the Three Levels at the Site and the Results of the Chi-square Test on these Values

| | Level 1 | | Level 2 | | Level 3 | | Total |
|---|---|---|---|---|---|---|---|
| | Observed | Expected | Observed | Expected | Observed | Expected | |
| Flakes with striking platforms.... | 36 | 39 | 37 | 37 | 17 | 15 | 90 |
| Flakes without striking platforms. | 60 | 79 | 85 | 76 | 40 | 30 | 185 |
| Block fracture flakes......... | 295 | 273 | 251 | 260 | 90 | 102 | 636 |
| Total....... | 391 | | 373 | | 147 | | 911 |

$\chi^2 = 12.94$ df = 4 $p < .02$

$\phi^2 = .014$

TABLE 29

FLAKES AND LEVELS

Observed and Expected Numbers of Small Retouch Flakes and all other Flake Types (Grouped) Found in the Three Levels at the Site and the Results of the Chi-square Test on these Values

| | Level 1 | | Level 2 | | Level 3 | | Total |
|---|---|---|---|---|---|---|---|
| | Observed | Expected | Observed | Expected | Observed | Expected | |
| Small retouch flakes........ | 1457 | 1475 | 1223 | 1273 | 917 | 849 | 3597 |
| All other flake types ........ | 391 | 373 | 373 | 323 | 147 | 215 | 911 |
| Total...... | 1848 | | 1596 | | 1064 | | 4508 |

$\chi^2 = 36.75$ df = 2 $p < .001$

$\phi^2 = .008$

in the case of the large flakes, the difference is barely significant ($p < .02$). Where the difference in size is large, as between the large flake groups and the small retouch flakes, this trend is more evident ($p < .001$). This might serve as another example of how surface collections could bias a sample away from small flakes.

In our quantitative examination of projectile point bases we noted a tendency for more than the expected numbers of white Bayport chert bases to be found in level three. This was not true for the dèbitage nor for the total sample of artifacts from the site.

The observed and expected distribution of chert types among

the dèbitage from the three levels at the site is given in Table 30. The chi-square value was not significant. We would expect this much variation between 40 and 50 per cent of the time by chance alone.

When the entire series of artifacts, including the point bases, was considered (Table 31) there again was no association between chert type and level. The amount of variation here would be expected by chance alone between 40 and 50 per cent of the time.

In light of the small sample of bases from level three and the results of the above two tests, I feel that there is no significant difference in chert between the various levels at the site.

TABLE 30

CHERT TYPE AND LEVEL

Observed and Expected Numbers of the Four Chert Categories among the Dèbitage in the Three Levels at the Site and the Results of the Chi-square Test on these Values

| | Level 1 | | Level 2 | | Level 3 | | Total |
|---|---|---|---|---|---|---|---|
| | Observed | Expected | Observed | Expected | Observed | Expected | |
| White Bayport . . . | 499 | 496 | 447 | 428 | 264 | 286 | 1210 |
| Light grey Bayport | 763 | 756 | 626 | 653 | 455 | 435 | 1844 |
| Dark grey Bayport | 524 | 524 | 456 | 453 | 298 | 301 | 1278 |
| Exotic material . . | 62 | 72 | 67 | 62 | 47 | 42 | 176 |
| Total . . . . . . | 1848 | | 1596 | | 1064 | | 4508 |

$\chi^2 = 7.08$ df = 6 p <.95

$\phi^2 = .002$

TABLE 31

CHERT TYPE AND LEVEL

Observed and Expected Numbers of the Four Chert Categories among the Artifacts Found in the Three Levels at the Site and the Results of the Chi-square Test on these Values

| | Level 1 | | Level 2 | | Level 3 | | Total |
|---|---|---|---|---|---|---|---|
| | Observed | Expected | Observed | Expected | Observed | Expected | |
| White Bayport . . . | 12 | 17 | 11 | 9 | 8 | 5 | 31 |
| Light grey Bayport | 46 | 41 | 19 | 20 | 8 | 12 | 73 |
| Dark grey Bayport | 15 | 15 | 6 | 7 | 5 | 4 | 26 |
| Exotic material . . | 2 | 2 | 1 | 1 | 0 | 0 | 3 |
| Total . . . . . . | 75 | | 37 | | 21 | | 133 |

$\chi^2 = 6.10$ df = 6 p <.50

$\phi^2 = .046$

We have information on the level in which 133 artifacts were found at the site. We could not test for all subgroups of artifacts since the sample was too small to fill all the cells with large enough numbers to make any valid tests. Therefore, the artifacts were grouped into three categories: complete or fragmentary preforms (31), complete and fragmentary finished bifaces (82) and a catchall category of all other artifacts (20).

The observed and expected distribution of these artifact groups in the three levels from the site is given in Table 32. There is very little difference between the observed and expected chance distribution. In fact, we would expect more variation by chance alone 90 per cent of the time. Therefore, there is no apparent temporal significance to these artifact types at the site.

The over-all picture from the vertical distribution of the cultural material is one of uniformity, that of a single component site. Chert types and artifact types at the several levels can be attributed to a natural tendency for light flakes to settle or be trampled into the sand and not to any cultural or time difference.

TABLE 32

ARTIFACTS AND LEVELS

Observed and Expected Numbers of Preforms, Finished Bifaces and all other Artifact Types Found in the Three Levels at the Site and the Results of the Chi-square Test on these Values

| | Level 1 | | Level 2 | | Level 3 | | |
|---|---|---|---|---|---|---|---|
| | Observed | Expected | Observed | Expected | Observed | Expected | Total |
| Preforms | 15 | 17 | 10 | 9 | 6 | 5 | 31 |
| Finished bifaces | 47 | 46 | 22 | 23 | 13 | 13 | 82 |
| Other artifacts | 13 | 12 | 5 | 5 | 2 | 3 | 21 |
| Total | 75 | | 37 | | 21 | | 133 |

$\chi^2 = .8517$ df = 4 p <.95

$\phi^2 = .006$

## Areal Distribution

The possibility of areal concentrations of certain kinds of cultural material from the Holcombe site had been suggested from our first day at the site. DeVisscher had noted concentrations of surface material and these concentrations determined which areas of the site were to be excavated. Even while

TABLE 33

FLAKE TYPES AND EXCAVATION UNITS

The Numbers of Flakes of Bifacial Retouch, Block Fracture Flakes and Small Retouch Flakes Found in the Three Areas and Individual Excavation Units on the Site

| Units | Flakes with Striking Platforms | Flakes without Striking Platforms | Block Fracture Flakes | Small Retouch Flakes | Total |
|---|---|---|---|---|---|
| Area I | | | | | |
| 610-490 . . . . . . . . | . . | 9 | 83 | 206 | 298 |
| 610-500 . . . . . . . . | 4 | 21 | 226 | 260 | 511 |
| 615-515 . . . . . . . . | . . | . . | 4 | 13 | 17 |
| 620-460 . . . . . . . . | . . | 1 | 1 | 22 | 24 |
| 620-470 . . . . . . . . | 2 | 4 | 18 | 63 | 87 |
| 620-480 . . . . . . . . | 10 | 22 | 31 | 217 | 280 |
| 620-490 . . . . . . . . | 14 | 29 | 93 | 580 | 716 |
| 620-500 . . . . . . . . | 14 | 24 | 127 | 333 | 498 |
| 620-510 . . . . . . . . | 5 | 4 | 16 | 95 | 120 |
| 630-470 . . . . . . . . | . . | . . | 6 | 21 | 27 |
| 630-480 . . . . . . . . | 2 | 11 | 10 | 70 | 93 |
| 630-490 . . . . . . . . | 4 | 11 | 21 | 111 | 147 |
| 630-500 . . . . . . . . | 13 | 9 | 30 | 454 | 506 |
| 630-510 . . . . . . . . | 2 | 1 | 14 | 87 | 104 |
| 640-490 . . . . . . . . | . . | 3 | 12 | 22 | 37 |
| Total . . . . . . . | 70 | 149 | 692 | 2554 | 3465 |
| Area II | | | | | |
| 570-530 . . . . . . . . | . . | 2 | 2 | 33 | 37 |
| 570-540 . . . . . . . . | 5 | 1 | 1 | 83 | 90 |
| 570-550 . . . . . . . . | 2 | 5 | 1 | 62 | 70 |
| *580-540 . . . . . . . . | 1 | 4 | 3 | 434 | 442 |
| †590-540 . . . . . . . . | 6 | 18 | 6 | 622 | 652 |
| 600-540 . . . . . . . . | 1 | 5 | 1 | 68 | 75 |
| Total . . . . . . . | 15 | 35 | 14 | 1302 | 1366 |
| Area III | | | | | |
| 120-100 . . . . . . . . | . . | 3 | 2 | 47 | 52 |
| 140-100 . . . . . . . . | . . | . . | . . | 13 | 13 |
| 570-490 . . . . . . . . | 4 | 5 | 3 | 72 | 84 |
| 570-500 . . . . . . . . | . . | 9 | 1 | 19 | 29 |
| Total . . . . . . . | 4 | 17 | 6 | 151 | 178 |

*One small potsherd weighing .3 grams was found in this unit.
†Two small potsherds with a total weight of .4 grams were found in this unit.

TABLE 34

CHERT TYPES AND EXCAVATION UNITS

The Frequencies of the Four Chert Classifications among the Debitage Found in the Three Areas and Individual Excavation Units on the Site

| Units | White Bayport | Light Grey Bayport | Dark Grey Bayport | Exotic Material | Total |
|---|---|---|---|---|---|
| Area I | | | | | |
| 610-490 . . . . . . . | 99 | 86 | 108 | 5 | 298 |
| 610-500 . . . . . . . | 179 | 158 | 171 | 3 | 511 |
| 615-515 . . . . . . . | 4 | 6 | 6 | 1 | 17 |
| 620-460 . . . . . . . | 7 | 10 | 7 | . . | 24 |
| 620-470 . . . . . . . | 20 | 28 | 31 | 8 | 87 |
| 620-480 . . . . . . . | 78 | 77 | 63 | 62 | 280 |
| 620-490 . . . . . . . | 204 | 259 | 209 | 44 | 716 |
| 620-500 . . . . . . . | 138 | 182 | 175 | 3 | 498 |
| 620-510 . . . . . . . | 29 | 62 | 24 | 5 | 120 |
| 630-470 . . . . . . . | 7 | 14 | 6 | 0 | 27 |
| 630-480 . . . . . . . | 37 | 26 | 20 | 10 | 93 |
| 630-490 . . . . . . . | 52 | 51 | 41 | 3 | 147 |
| 630-500 . . . . . . . | 101 | 244 | 160 | 1 | 506 |
| 630-510 . . . . . . . | 14 | 57 | 30 | 3 | 104 |
| 640-490 . . . . . . . | 11 | 14 | 12 | . . | 37 |
| Total . . . . . . | 980 | 1273 | 1064 | 148 | 3465 |
| Area II | | | | | |
| 570-530 . . . . . . . | 4 | 26 | 7 | . . | 37 |
| 570-540 . . . . . . . | 9 | 54 | 22 | 5 | 90 |
| 570-550 . . . . . . . | 13 | 30 | 19 | 8 | 70 |
| *580-540 . . . . . . . | 104 | 243 | 80 | 15 | 442 |
| †590-540 . . . . . . . | 117 | 343 | 175 | 17 | 652 |
| 600-540 . . . . . . . | 16 | 39 | 13 | 7 | 75 |
| Total . . . . . . | 263 | 735 | 316 | 52 | 1366 |
| Area III | | | | | |
| 120-100 . . . . . . . | 36 | 12 | 4 | . . | 52 |
| 140-100 . . . . . . . | 5 | 5 | 3 | . . | 13 |
| 570-490 . . . . . . . | 12 | 49 | 22 | 1 | 84 |
| 570-500 . . . . . . . | 3 | 17 | 6 | 3 | 29 |
| Total . . . . . . | 56 | 83 | 35 | 4 | 178 |

*One small potsherd weighing .3 grams was found in this unit.
†Two small potsherds with a total weight of .4 grams were found in this unit.

excavating the site it became evident that the sheer quantity of material recovered from some areas was greater than that from other areas. In the laboratory, qualitative as well as quantitative differences between excavation units were examined.

There were over 4,000 pieces of dèbitage from excavated areas. Sixty-one pieces came from the four scattered excavation units and will be excluded from the rest of this analysis. The numbers and types of flakes recovered from the excavated areas on the site are given in Table 33 and the chert types are given in Table 34.

Out of the 25 excavation units listed in Tables 33 and 34 only 11 contained more than 100 pieces of dèbitage. These were the areas of concentration on the site and it was decided that they would be the units used for detailed comparisons. It can be noted that nine of these units cluster around unit 620-500 in Area I. The other two are adjacent units in Area II. None of the units in Area III produced enough dèbitage to be used in this comparison.

In order to compare the flakes from these units the raw counts were reduced to percentages which were plotted on a cumulative graph. The graph with eleven lines was cluttered but it was obvious that there were four distinct clusters of nearly parallel lines. These four groups and the percentages of the groups are presented in Table 35. This table provides information which can be plotted on a cumulative graph using the grouped data (Figure 10).

In the New World the cumulative graph has been used for temporal ordering of archaeological material (Jelinek, 1962). In this instance, however, I feel that the flake-type profiles shown in the cumulative graph represent functional differences between the units on the site. Groups I and II represent areas where primary working and preform preparation were carried out. They are high in block fracture flakes and have moderate numbers of flakes of bifacial retouch. Group IV has moderate numbers of block fracture flakes and relatively high numbers of small retouch flakes. Group III has only an average three per cent block fracture flakes and over 90 per cent small retouch flakes. Groups III and IV seem to represent units where pressure retouch work was being carried out.

Since nine of these units form a cluster in Area I the distribution of these flake groups was easy to plot (Figure 11). Groups I and II were found in three contiguous units, surrounded on three sides by six units with Group III and IV flake-type profiles. The

TABLE 35

FLAKE GROUPS

Percentages of Flakes of Bifacial Retouch, Block Fracture Flakes and Small Retouch Flakes among Flake Groups with the Percentage for each Unit and the Average for the Group

| Groups and Units | Flakes with Striking Platforms (Per Cent) | Flakes without Striking Platforms (Per Cent) | Block Fracture Flakes (Per Cent) | Small Retouch Flakes (Per Cent) | N |
|---|---|---|---|---|---|
| Group I | | | | | |
| 610-500 ....... | 1 | 4 | 44 | 51 | 511 |
| Average ....... | 1 | 4 | 44 | 51 | |
| Group II | | | | | |
| 610-490 ....... | .. | 3 | 28 | 69 | 298 |
| 620-500 ....... | 3 | 5 | 26 | 66 | 498 |
| Average ....... | 2 | 4 | 27 | 67 | |
| Group III | | | | | |
| 580-540 ....... | .. | 1 | 1 | 98 | 442 |
| 590-540 ....... | 1 | 3 | 1 | 96 | 652 |
| 630-500 ....... | 2 | 2 | 6 | 90 | 506 |
| Average ....... | 1 | 2 | 3 | 94 | |
| Group IV | | | | | |
| 620-480 ....... | 4 | 8 | 11 | 77 | 280 |
| 620-490 ....... | 2 | 4 | 13 | 81 | 716 |
| 620-510 ....... | 4 | 3 | 13 | 79 | 120 |
| 630-490 ....... | 3 | 7 | 14 | 76 | 147 |
| 630-510 ....... | 2 | 1 | 13 | 84 | 104 |
| Average ....... | 3 | 5 | 13 | 79 | |

two units in Area II fall into Group III, the group with the highest percentage of small retouch flakes.

The interpretation given to this pattern of distribution is that there was a central area where primary flint working was carried out surrounded by an area where artifacts were repaired and finished.

The chert distribution was analyzed in the same manner. The units with over one-hundred pieces of dèbitage were compared in terms of percentages of chert variants on a cumulative graph.

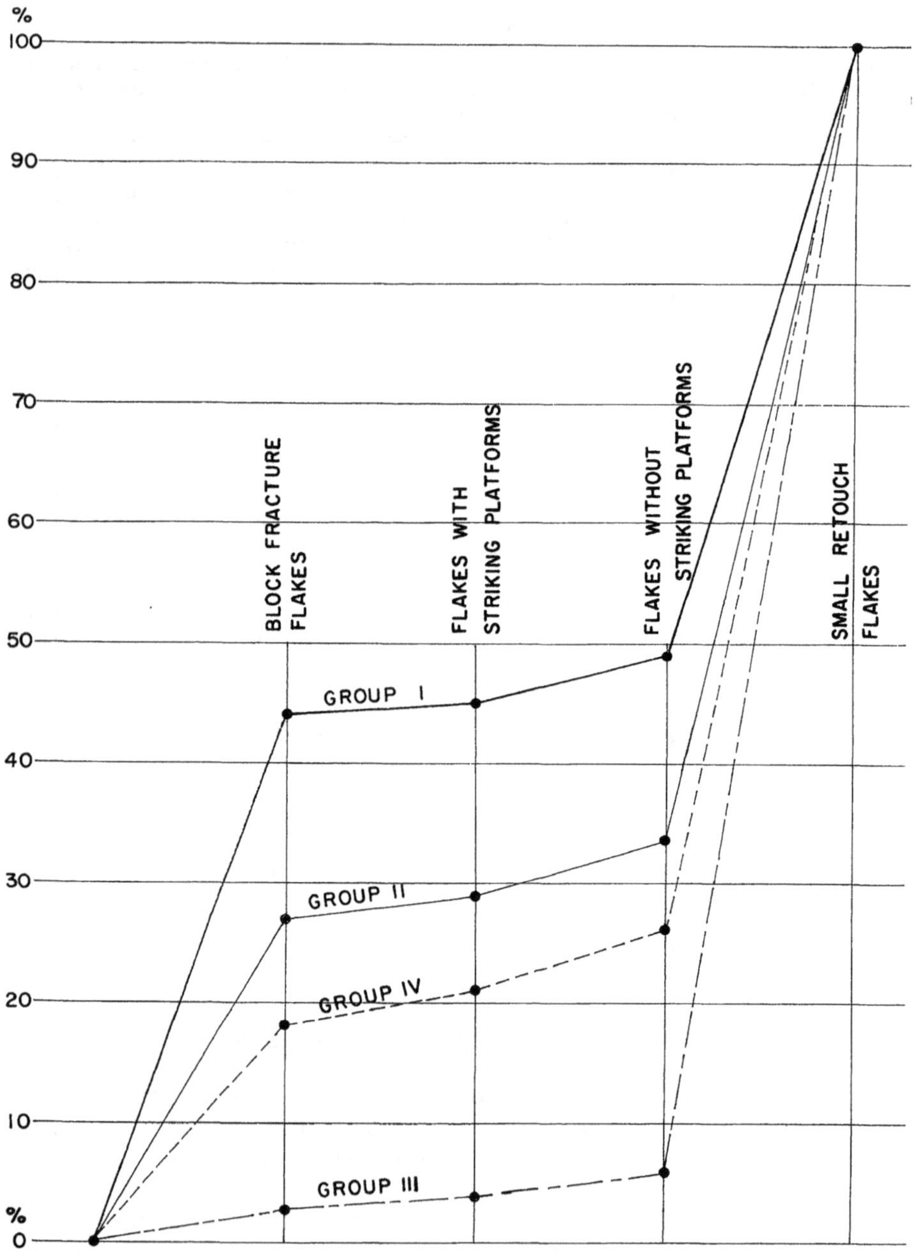


FIG. 10. Cumulative graph of flake-type groups from the Holcombe site.

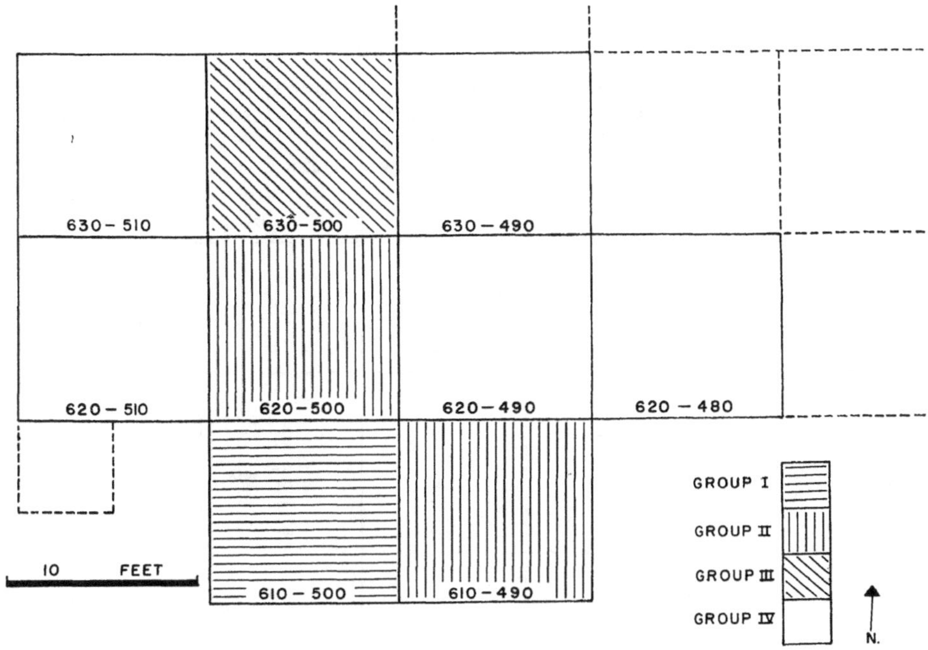


FIG. 11. Distribution of flake groups in high concentration units at the Holcombe site (minimal N per unit = 100).

It was obvious that there were distinct differences in chert distribution. An examination of Table 34 shows that units 620-480 and 620-490 contain 72 per cent of the exotic chert in Area I. These two units contain 42 per cent of the entire sample of exotic chert from the site found by both DeVisscher and the University of Michigan. Unit 620-480 alone contains 25 per cent of all the exotic chert found on the site. Exotic material accounts for 22 per cent of all the chert in this unit but only 3 per cent of the dèbitage from the site.

This exotic grouping was readily reflected in the cumulative graph. Other groups seemed to be present but not as obviously. It was possible to recognize four groups of units which had similar percentage profiles. These groups, the percentages, and the average percentage for each group are given in Table 36. When the mean percentages of these groups were plotted on a cumulative graph (Figure 12) some difference could be seen. Group I was high in exotic material. Group II is characterized by large

TABLE 36

CHERT GROUPS

Percentages of the Four Chert Classifications among the Débitage for Chert Groups with the Percentage for each Unit and the Average for each Group

| Groups and Units | White Bayport (Per Cent) | Light Grey Bayport (Per Cent) | Dark Grey Bayport (Per Cent) | Exotic Material (Per Cent) | N |
|---|---|---|---|---|---|
| Group I | | | | | |
| 620-480 ....... | 28 | 27 | 23 | 22 | 280 |
| Average ....... | 28 | 27 | 23 | 22 | |
| Group II | | | | | |
| 590-540 ....... | 18 | 53 | 27 | 2 | 652 |
| 630-500 ....... | 20 | 48 | 32 | .. | 506 |
| 630-510 ....... | 13 | 55 | 29 | 3 | 104 |
| Average ....... | 17 | 52 | 29 | 2 | |
| Group III | | | | | |
| 580-540 ....... | 24 | 55 | 18 | 3 | 442 |
| 620-510 ....... | 24 | 52 | 20 | 4 | 120 |
| Average ....... | 24 | 53 | 19 | 4 | |
| Group IV | | | | | |
| 610-490 ....... | 33 | 29 | 36 | 2 | 298 |
| 610-500 ....... | 35 | 31 | 33 | 1 | 511 |
| 620-490 ....... | 29 | 36 | 29 | 6 | 716 |
| 620-500 ....... | 27 | 37 | 35 | 1 | 498 |
| 630-490 ....... | 35 | 35 | 28 | 2 | 147 |
| Average ....... | 32 | 34 | 32 | 2 | |

amounts of both light grey and dark grey Bayport chert while Group III is marked by high amounts of light grey Bayport chert and almost equal amounts of dark grey and white Bayport chert. The three Bayport chert variants are found in almost equal numbers in Group IV.

The units in these various groups in the central area are marked in Figure 13. Again we have a central area which, in this instance, incorporated five units. This area is surrounded on three sides by units containing distinctive chert profiles.

When the chert and flake maps are combined from the core area in Area I a distinctive pattern emerges. The units which

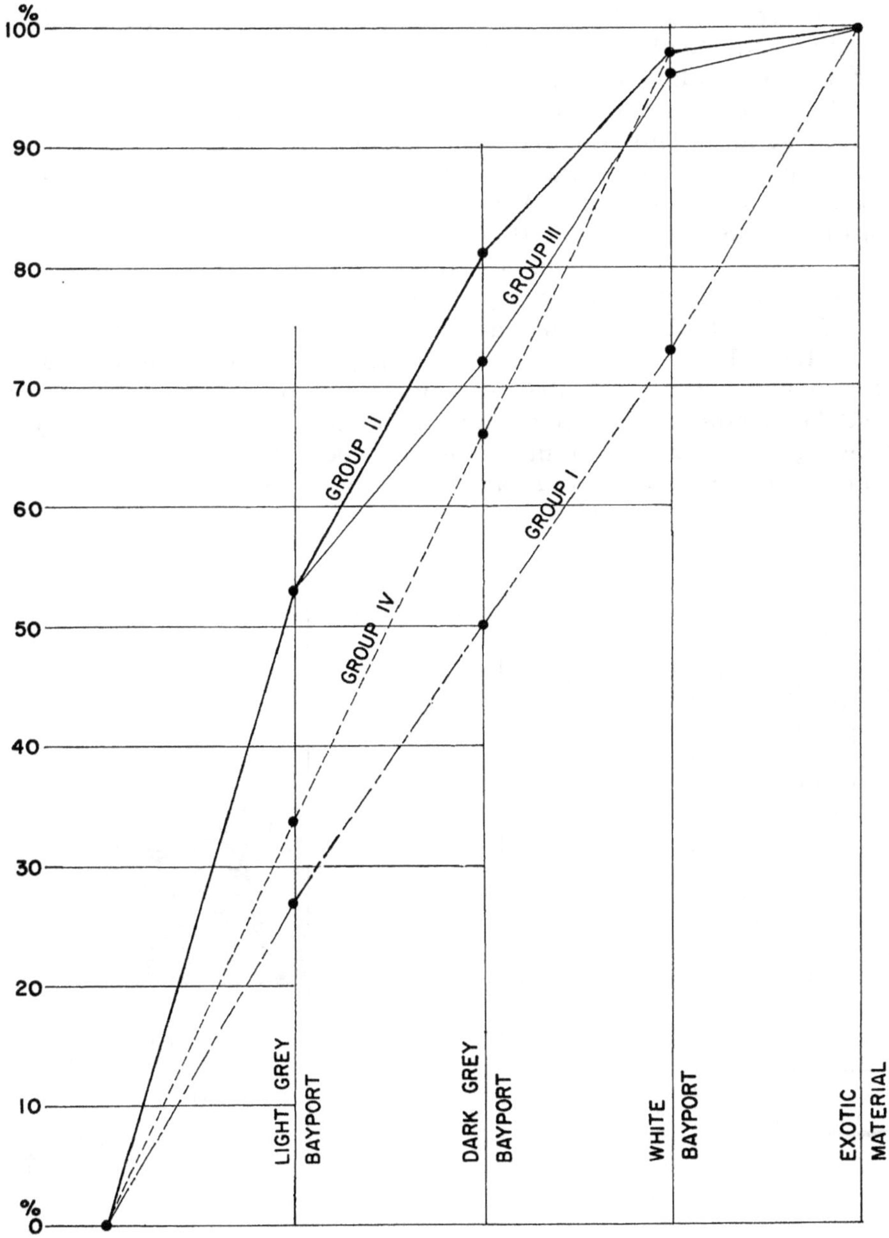


FIG. 12. Cumulative graph showing chert groups among the dèbitage from the Holcombe site.

were defined as primary flint-working areas contain almost equal percentages of all the Bayport chert variants. The areas where retouch and repair of artifacts took place are marked by distinctive and individual chert profiles.

Feature Number 2 was located in unit 620-500 in the center of this group. This feature was marked by an extraordinarily high number of block fracture flakes. Virtually all of the calcined animal bone found below the plow zone came from this feature. One fragment of this calcined bone has been identified as barren-ground caribou, a fairly large animal which would serve as food for a number of people.

This central area may have been a communal area on the site where large animals, killed in a group-hunting effort, were cooked and eaten. The preparation of preforms, which might also have been held in common since a hunter would have no way of knowing when or how many tools he would lose or break, was carried out in this central area. When a man was finishing his

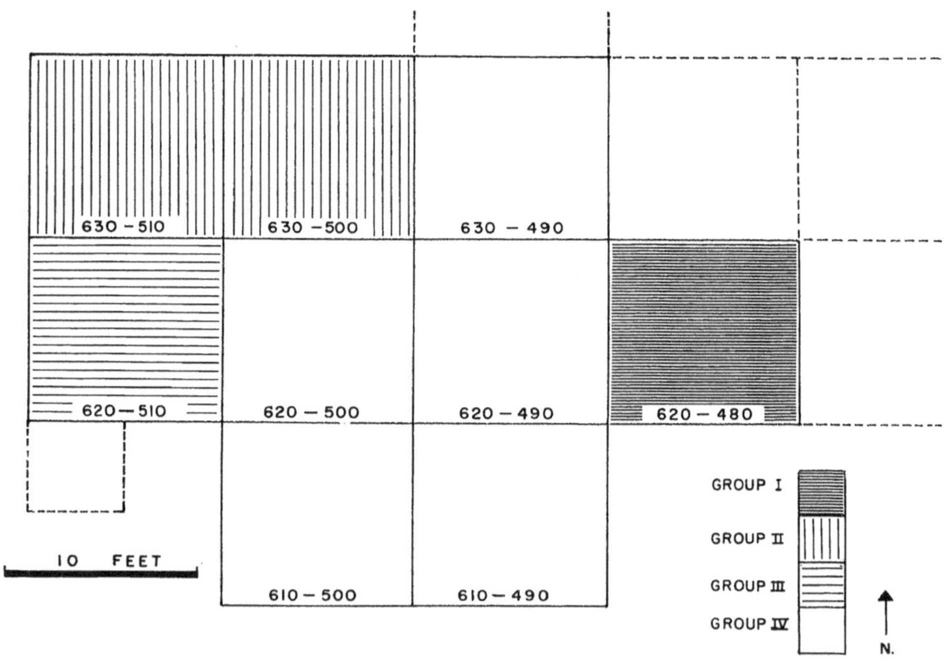


FIG. 13. Distribution of chert groups among dèbitage from high concentration units at the Holcombe site (minimal N per unit = 100).

tools or resharpening them he left the central area and returned to the family group. These family groups were scattered around the communal area on the site. In these areas surrounding the communal area we found excavation units with many small retouch flakes and distinctive chert profiles. The chert profiles represent the raw material preference of the individual knappers.

We also have another type of feature at the site—the feature with almost no cultural material. Features Number 1, 4, and 8 were very similar to Feature Number 2 in form but lacked the cultural material and calcined bone fragments. Features Number 1 and 8 are in the areas of more than one-hundred pieces of dèbitage. Feature Number 8 is completely in a retouch area while Feature Number 1 overlaps a retouch area and a primary flint-working area. It is possible that these were areas where individual family groups built small fires to provide warmth. They contain no animal bone to suggest food preparation such as we noted in Feature Number 2.

The distribution of artifacts on the site bears out the interpretation derived from a study of the dèbitage. The differences are not as distinctive because of the smaller sample size, less than 150 artifacts as opposed to over 4,000 pieces of dèbitage.

The artifacts were divided into the three groups which were used for the study of vertical distribution: preforms, finished bifaces and all other artifacts. The numbers and percentages of these artifacts for the three areas on the site are given in Table 37. For comparative purposes we used only units with seven or more artifacts. The only two categories which were plotted were units having more than 40 per cent preforms and units having more than 40 per cent finished bifaces (Figure 14).

The units which are high in preforms, 610-500 and 620-500, are the same units which were high in block fracture flakes. This is further evidence for the contention that block fracture flakes resulted from the technique used in preform preparation. All of the surrounding units contained more than 40 per cent finished bifaces and less than 40 per cent preforms.

The numbers and percentages of the several chert classifications among the artifacts are recorded in Table 38. These were plotted using three categories: more than 40 per cent white Bayport chert, more than 40 per cent light grey Bayport chert, and more than 40 per cent dark grey Bayport chert. All units with less than seven artifacts were excluded.

When this material was plotted (Figure 15) the high concentrations of dark grey artifacts were found in units 610-500 and

TABLE 37

ARTIFACTS AND EXCAVATION UNITS

The Number and Percentages of Preforms, Finished Bifaces and other Artifacts Found in the Three Areas and Individual Excavation Units on the Site

| Units | Preforms | | Finished Bifaces | | Other Artifacts | | Total |
|---|---|---|---|---|---|---|---|
| | N | Per Cent | N | Per Cent | N | Per Cent | |
| Area I | | | | | | | |
| 610-490 . . . . . . | 3 | 27 | 7 | 64 | 1 | 9 | 11 |
| 610-500 . . . . . . | 4 | 57 | 3 | 43 | . . | . . | 7 |
| 615-515 . . . . . . | . . | . . | . . | . . | 1 | 100 | 1 |
| 620-460 . . . . . . | 1 | 33 | 1 | 33 | 1 | 33 | 3 |
| 620-470 . . . . . . | 1 | 20 | 4 | 80 | . . | . . | 5 |
| 620-480 . . . . . . | 1 | 8 | 9 | 75 | 2 | 17 | 12 |
| 620-490 . . . . . . | 4 | 21 | 14 | 74 | 1 | 5 | 19 |
| 620-500 . . . . . . | 7 | 47 | 7 | 47 | 1 | 6 | 15 |
| 620-510 . . . . . . | 1 | 11 | 4 | 44 | 4 | 44 | 9 |
| 630-470 . . . . . . | . . | . . | . . | . . | 1 | 100 | 1 |
| 630-480 . . . . . . | 3 | 43 | 3 | 43 | 1 | 14 | 7 |
| 630-490 . . . . . . | 2 | 20 | 5 | 50 | 3 | 30 | 10 |
| 630-500 . . . . . . | 1 | 14 | 6 | 86 | . . | . . | 7 |
| 630-510 . . . . . . | 1 | 50 | 1 | 50 | . . | . . | 2 |
| 640-490 . . . . . . | 1 | 100 | . . | . . | . . | . . | 1 |
| Total . . . . . | 30 | | 64 | | 16 | | 110 |
| Area II | | | | | | | |
| 570-530 . . . . . . | . . | . . | . . | . . | . . | . . | . . |
| 570-540 . . . . . . | 1 | 50 | 1 | 50 | . . | . . | 2 |
| 570-550 . . . . . . | 1 | 33 | 2 | 67 | . . | . . | 3 |
| *580-540 . . . . . . | 1 | 12 | 6 | 75 | 1 | 12 | 8 |
| †590-540 . . . . . . | . . | . . | 5 | 71 | 2 | 29 | 7 |
| 600-540 . . . . . . | . . | . . | . . | . . | 1 | 100 | 1 |
| Total . . . . . | 3 | | 14 | | 4 | | 21 |
| Area III | | | | | | | |
| 120-100 . . . . . . | . . | . . | 2 | 100 | . . | . . | 2 |
| 140-100 . . . . . . | . . | . . | 1 | 100 | . . | . . | 1 |
| 570-490 . . . . . . | . . | . . | 2 | 100 | . . | . . | 2 |
| 570-500 . . . . . . | . . | . . | . . | . . . | . . | . . | . . |
| Total . . . . . | . . | | 5 | | . . | | 5 |

*One small potsherd weighing .3 grams was found in this unit.
†Two small potsherds with a total weight of .4 grams were found in this unit.

TABLE 38

CHERT TYPES AND EXCAVATION UNITS

The Numbers and Percentages of the Four Chert Categories among the Artifacts for the Three Areas and Individual Excavation Units on the Site

| Units | White Bayport | | Light Grey Bayport | | Dark Grey Bayport | | Exotic Material | | Total |
|---|---|---|---|---|---|---|---|---|---|
| | N | Per Cent | N | Per Cent | N | Per Cent | N | Per Cent | |
| Area I | | | | | | | | | |
| 610-490 . . . . . . . | 5 | 45 | 3 | 27 | 3 | 27 | . . | . . | 11 |
| 610-500 . . . . . . . | 1 | 14 | 3 | 43 | 3 | 43 | . . | . . | 7 |
| 615-515 . . . . . . . | . . | . . | 1 | 100 | . . | . . | . . | . . | 1 |
| 620-460 . . . . . . . | 1 | 33 | 2 | 67 | . . | . . | . . | . . | 3 |
| 620-470 . . . . . . . | . . | . . | 4 | 80 | 1 | 20 | . . | . . | 5 |
| 620-480 . . . . . . . | 3 | 25 | 7 | 58 | 2 | 17 | . . | . . | 12 |
| 620-490 . . . . . . . | 4 | 21 | 11 | 58 | 4 | 21 | . . | . . | 19 |
| 620-500 . . . . . . . | 3 | 20 | 6 | 40 | 6 | 40 | . . | . . | 15 |
| 620-510 . . . . . . . | 4 | 44 | 3 | 33 | 2 | 22 | . . | . . | 9 |
| 630-470 . . . . . . . | . . | . . | 1 | 100 | . . | . . | . . | . . | 1 |
| 630-480 . . . . . . . | 3 | 43 | 3 | 43 | 1 | 14 | . . | . . | 7 |
| 630-490 . . . . . . . | 3 | 30 | 4 | 40 | 1 | 10 | 2 | 20 | 10 |
| 630-500 . . . . . . . | 2 | 29 | 5 | 71 | . . | . . | . . | . . | 7 |
| 630-510 . . . . . . . | . . | . . | 1 | 50 | 1 | 50 | . . | . . | 2 |
| 640-490 . . . . . . . | . . | . . | . . | . . . | 1 | 100 | . . | . . | 1 |
| Total . . . . . . | 29 | | 54 | | 25 | | 2 | | 110 |
| Area II | | | | | | | | | |
| 570-530 . . . . . . . | . . | . . | . . | . . . | . . | . . | . . | . . | . . |
| 570-540 . . . . . . . | . . | . . | 2 | 100 | . . | . . | . . | . . | 2 |
| 570-550 . . . . . . . | . . | . . | 2 | 67 | . . | . . | 1 | 33 | 3 |
| *580-540 . . . . . . . | . . | . . | 7 | 88 | 1 | 12 | . . | . . | 8 |
| †590-540 . . . . . . . | . . | . . | 5 | 71 | 2 | 29 | . . | . . | 7 |
| 600-540 . . . . . . . | . . | . . | 1 | 100 | . . | . . | . . | . . | 1 |
| Total . . . . . . | . . | | 17 | | 3 | | 1 | | 21 |
| Area III | | | | | | | | | |
| 120-100 . . . . . . . | 1 | 50 | . . | . . . | 1 | 50 | . . | . . | 2 |
| 140-100 . . . . . . . | 1 | 100 | . . | . . . | . . | . . | . . | . . | 1 |
| 570-490 . . . . . . . | . . | . . . | 2 | 100 | . . | . . | . . | . . | 2 |
| 570-500 . . . . . . . | . . | . . . | . . | . . . | . . | . . | . . | . . | . . |
| Total . . . . . . | 2 | | 2 | | 1 | | . . | | 5 |

*One small potsherd weighing .3 grams was found in this unit.
†Two small potsherds with a total weight of .4 grams were found in this unit.

620-500, the same areas which contained the most dark grey dèbitage. Surrounding these units are areas with fairly distinctive chert profiles.

While the sample of artifacts was too small to be significant by itself, it does add weight to the settlement organization suggested by the distribution of the dèbitage.

While the vertical distribution of cultural material at the site indicates little or no cultural difference between levels, there do

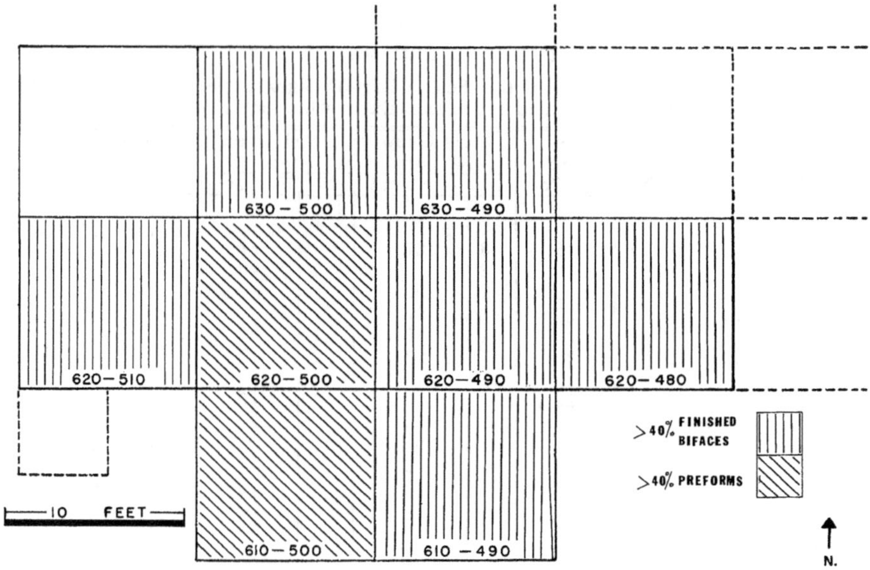


FIG. 14. Artifact distribution from high concentration units at the Holcombe site (minimal N per unit = 7).

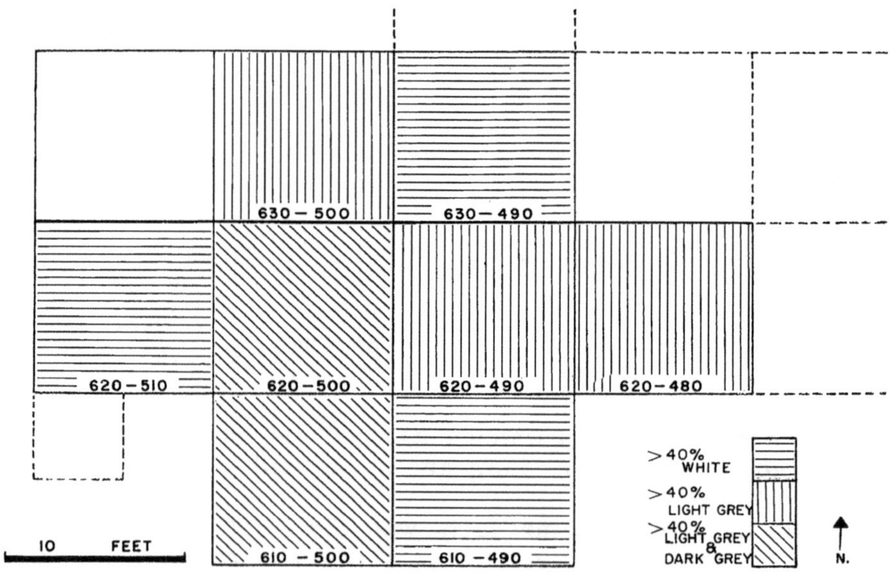


FIG. 15. Chert distribution of artifacts from high concentration units at the Holcombe site (minimal N per unit = 7).

appear to be differences between units with much cultural material and those with a lesser amount of dèbris. It is possible to define a core area on the site where the main Paleo-Indian occupation occurred. Within this core area there appears to be a communal area where food preparation took place, at least for large game. The initial working and heat-treating of preforms also took place here. Surrounding this communal area are areas which appear to have been occupied by individual families. These areas are marked by a high occurrence of small retouch flakes indicating finishing or repair of artifacts, distinctive chert profiles reflecting individual family chert preferences, and fired areas without calcined animal bone or dèbitage which could be interpreted as fires built by the family units for warmth.

Five such areas were present in the areas excavated by the University of Michigan at the Holcombe site and we could postulate three more to complete the symmetry of the camp. If we take the minimum concentration number of 5 and a minimum family size of 4 individuals in each unit the total population of the Holcombe site was 20 individuals. Taking the maximum number of possible family units, estimated at 8, and a higher estimate of 6 individuals in each family unit, we could postulate a population of 48 individuals in the camp. The actual band size was probably somewhere between 20 and 50 people.

The group which occupied the area of the Holcombe site over 11,000 years ago appears to have been typical of hunting and gathering bands. There were 5 to 8 males and their families in the group. These caribou hunters stayed for a short time while the hunting was good. They repaired and refinished their spears and then moved on in their seasonal pattern.

## PART II

# OTHER PALEO-INDIAN SITES ALONG THE HOLCOMBE BEACH

*Jerry DeVisscher and Edward J. Wahla*

## V

### THE DEVISSCHER PALEO-II OCCUPATION SITE

The second Early Man site along the Holcombe beach was discovered by Mr. Jerry DeVisscher of Mt. Clemens, finder of the Holcombe site. It is located in the southeast quarter of the southwest quarter of section 23, Sterling Township, Macomb County, Michigan, and is 64 rods north of Sixteen Mile Road, at the midsection line fence.

The new site was rather small. It was dug by DeVisscher with the occasional help of Edward J. Wahla and other members of the Aboriginal Research Club of Detroit and the Michigan Archaeological Society. Work was begun during the fall of 1961 and continued intermittently during the summer and fall of 1962. The site was worked in five-foot squares to accommodate a part-time schedule. The upper plow zone was screened with the aid of a mechanical sifter, the lower portions carefully troweled for any possible features or artifacts *in situ.* No diagnostic features were present, and no true stratification was observable; all artifacts were either in the plow zone or just below it. The total site covered a 65- by 75-foot area with noticeable concentrations. There was virtually no evidence of multiple occupation although various sites of later cultures are to be found on the same large ridge, one beginning at the south edge of the site where two tiny scraps of pottery and a stemmed point were picked up on the surface.

The site is situated on a 610-foot fossil beach, part of a long sandspit which was a feature of the ancient Lake Clinton shoreline. It is one-half mile east of the Holcombe site and on the same ridge. The area is so sandy that an old, standing wire fence at the east margin is entirely duned over. The difficulty of working such a site can be imagined. The field east of the fence had been stripped of sand and probably some of the occupation area was destroyed. Tiny, characteristic "paleo-flakes" can still be found there.

While the ratio of broken spear bases to whole unaltered blades on the Holcombe site was about 50 to 1, a much lower ratio was found at Paleo-II. Here 10 whole or major portions of blades and 18 basal fragments were excavated. This is an exceptional number of whole points for a small site, but it must be noted that only 3 are undamaged (possibly lost specimens, the others being damaged or rejects).

The presence of basal stubs without the corresponding distal parts indicates that the hunting spears had been rearmed in camp.

The spearheads were probably so nicely and securely bound (and perhaps cemented) in place that it was impractical to do the job in the field. The blades were apparently finished from preformed blanks on the site.

An important feature of these paleo-sites is the occurrence of thousands of small, almost microscopic, secondary flint flakes. Most of them pass through a 1/4-inch screen but some vary up to 5/8-inch. They are flat, fragile, and very thin, some less than .5 mm in thickness. There is an interesting type of larger spall which gives further evidence of the use of blanks for making spears. These were removed by percussion while thinning the blanks. The striking platform used was the original beveled edge of the blank, and enough remains to reveal the original angle. The dearth of rough spalls and scraps bears out the fact that few artifacts were made directly from nodules or quarry flint.

The thin, flat bifacial artifacts typical of this site, which resemble those from the Holcombe site, are referred to here also as "Holcombe points." Some blades, notably D-30, 32, 53, 9 and P2 have had tiny chips broken out of their edges above the lateral grinding. It is possible that this was caused by a heavy pull on the binding sinew above the point where the smoothing would have prevented it from catching on the thin, sharp edge.

Some of the blades show good collateral flaking, especially evident in the midsections. We get the impression from the better examples of "Holcombe" work that here is an elite product of eastern late Paleo-Indian flint workers. The Holcombe beach seems to produce a unique point, perhaps a type in itself.

Among other artifacts found in the excavation of the site were finely edge-flaked end scrapers, side scrapers and spokeshave scrapers, ovoid fragments of blanks, drills of rather unusual type, gravers, burins (?) and abrading stones.

Some small fragments and flakes of charcoal were present in both the plow zone and the area just below it. A few test pits dug a short distance away from the site yielded little charcoal so a great deal of time was spent collecting the charcoal from the deeper zone of the excavation. This may, however, be the residue of comparatively recent forest fires.

Photographic slides were made by Wahla and DeVisscher as the work progressed. The completed or unfinished points recovered from DeVisscher Paleo-II occupation site are shown in Figure 16 and Plate IX. Artifact designation numbers are those originally placed upon the item at time of excavation. Dimensions of points are given in millimeters. Abbreviations are as follows: L, total length; w, maximum width; wb, width at basal tangs; x, thickest point; o, thickness about 12 mm from base end; f, flute length; rf, flute length reverse face.

D-30. Damaged point. L: 68 mm - w: 26 mm - wb: 19 mm - x: 5 mm - 0: 3.5 mm - f: 14 mm - rf: hinge fracture at 7 mm. Figure 16, *b* ; Plate IX, *b* .

D-38. Body fragment. L: 43 mm - w: 22 mm - x: 5.5 mm. Figure 16, *i*; Plate IX, *i* .

D-9. Point with unground basal edges (unfinished?) L: 58 mm - w: 19 mm - wb: 18 mm - x: 6.5 mm - o: 3.5 mm - f: 12 mm - rf: 6 mm. Figure 16, *c*; Plate IX, *c*.

D-90. Good finished blade. L: 58 mm - w: 23 mm - wb: 20 mm - x: 5 mm - o: 2 mm - f: 19 mm multiple - rf: 20 mm multiple. Figure 16, *a*; Plate IX, *a*.

D-56. Apparently a point in process of manufacture. If so, the process is not in the order usually expected. The left edge is nicely worked, both faces. The long flake scars average 23 mm. Right side is original and unworked (or edge was sheared off) - L: 40 mm - w: 17 mm - x: 4.5 mm - o: 3.5 mm - f: 15 mm. Figure 16, *x;* Plate IX, *x*.

D-26. Parallel flakes body section. L: 45 mm - w: 26 mm - x: 4.5 mm. Figure 16, *g*; Plate IX, *g*.

D-35. The two parts of this fine blade were found 16 feet apart. L: 50 mm - w: 20 mm - x: 5 mm - o: 3 mm - f: 23 mm to break. rf: none - wb: 13 mm. Figure 16, *e* ; Plate IX, *e*.

D-1. Distal portion, base missing, site surface find. L: 50 mm - w: 25 mm - x: 6 mm.

D-53. Bilaterally symmetrical, fine "pumpkin seed"- shaped blade. L: 56 mm - w: 28 mm - wb: 16 mm - x: 4.5 mm - o: 3 mm - f: 13 mm - rf: bevel only. Extremely flat specimen. Figure 16, *d*; Plate IX, *d*.

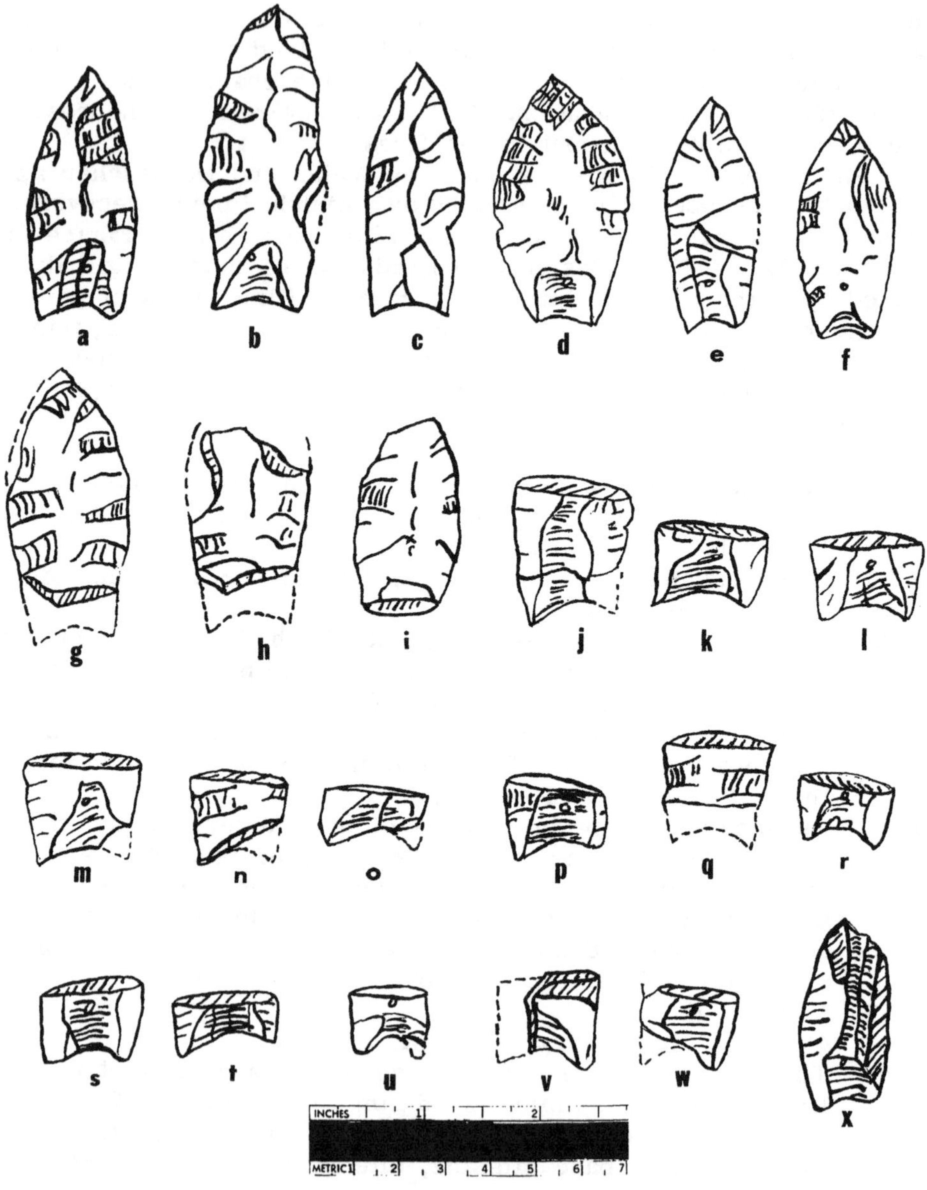


FIG. 16. Artifacts from Paleo-II. Projectile points and point fragments.

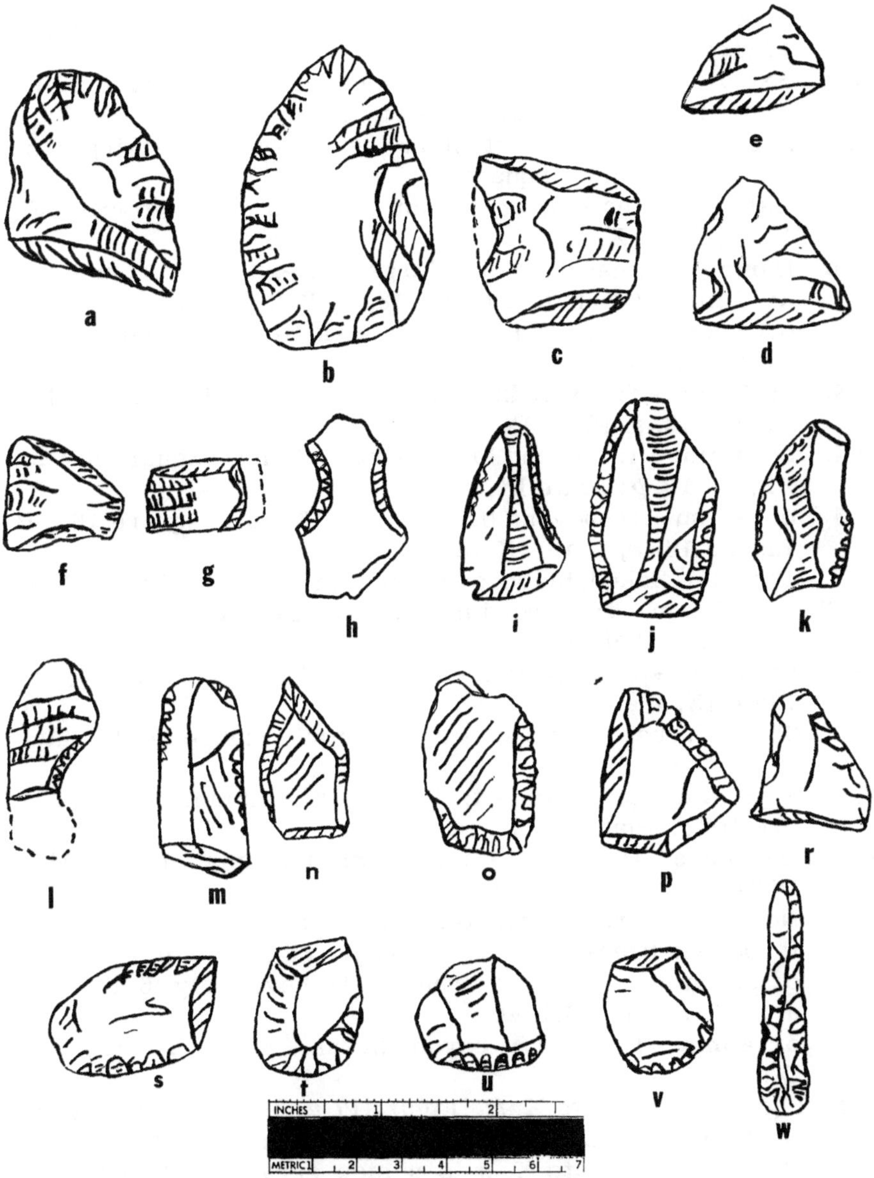

FIG. 17. Artifacts from Paleo-II. *a-d*, preforms; *f-g*, medial fragments; *h*, spokeshave scraper; *i-k*, scrapers; *l*, fragment of a spokeshave scraper; *m-v*, scrapers; *w*, drill.

D-32. Unfinished?, nonfluted blade showing flint core pattern; no grinding. L: 50 mm - w: 22 mm - x: 5 mm - o: 3.5 mm. Figure 16, *f*; Plate IX, *f*.

D-65. Excellent, ground edge, midsection. w: 27 mm - x: 5.5 mm - f: 9 mm remaining - rf: shattered.

D-25. Distal part of a chert blank, no secondary flaking. L: 52 mm - x: 8 mm - square.

D-3. Large midsection, w: 27 mm - x: 5.5 mm. Ground. Figure 17, *f*; Plate X, *f*.

D-34. Damaged midsection of a large well-made Holcombe point. x: 5 mm. Ground. Figure 16, *n*; Plate IX, *n*.

D-8. o: 4 mm - f: 15 mm - rf: face shattered. Figure 16, *m*; Plate IX, *m*.

D-74. o: 3 mm - f: extends beyond break - rf: 18 mm multiple. Figure 16, *i*; Plate IX, *i*.

D-54. o: 3 mm - f: beyond break - rf: 16 mm - Square 9 - C. Figure 16, *p*; Plate IX, *p*.

D-55. o: 3 mm - f: beyond break - rf: 16 mm - square 10 - B. Figure 16, *k*; Plate IX, *k*.

D-2. Parallel flaked blade section. Figure 16, *q*; Plate IX, *q*.

D-122. x: 4.5 mm - f: beyond break (over 31 mm) rf: 30 mm. Fig 16, *j*, Plate IX, *j*.

D-24. o: 3 mm - f: beyond break - rf: 14 mm. Figure 16, *s*; Plate IX, *s*.

D-4. Thin. f: beyond break - rf: 20 mm. Figure 16, *t*; Plate IX, *t*.

D-7. x: 4 mm - o: 3 mm - f: 7 mm - rf: 10 mm multiple. Figure 16, *v*; Plate IX, *v*.

D-6. Half base. f: 12 mm - rf: 10 mm multiple. Figure 16, *v*; Plate IX, *v*.

D-91. No flute scar. Figure 16, *n*; Plate IX, *n*.

D-60. f: beyond break - rf: bevel only. Figure 16, *o*; Plate IX, *o*.

D-65. o: 2.5 mm - f: beyond break - rf: bevel only, 6 mm. Figure 16, *w*; Plate IX, *w*.

D-80. o: 4 mm - f: and rf: beyond break. Figure 16, *v*; Plate IX, *v*.

D-43. Figure 17, *t*; Plate X, *t*: Figure 17, *u*; Plate X, *u*: Figure 17, *v*; Plate X, *v*: end scrapers made from select spalls.

D-58. Figure 17, *s*; Plate X, *s* is a side scraper with two worked edges.

D-10. Heavy knife or preform fragment. L: 55 mm - w: 37 mm - x: 8 mm. Has good secondary flaking. Figure 17, *a*; Plate X, *a*.

D-61. Fragment with parallel flake scars. Figure 17, *g*; Plate X, *g*.

D-11. Figure 17, *h*; Plate X, *h* and Figure 17, *i*; Plate X, *i* whole and fragmentary "spoke shaves." The radius of the curved face suggests the maximum diameter of the shaft worked on. Radii of Holcombe site spoke shave similar, about 1".

D-44. Figure 17, *i*; Plate X, *i*, Figure 17, *k*; Plate X, *k*, Figures 17, *j*; Plate X, *j*, Figure 17, *m*; Plate X, *m* are finely edge-flaked on both long edges.

D-33 is a flat, specialized scraper and/or graver of good workmanship. Figure 17, *n*; Plate X, *n*.

D-83. Figure 17, *p*; Plate X, *p* and Figure 17, *o*; Plate X, *o* are scrapers from rough spalls.

D-112 and 80, are thin spalls showing only casual edge working. Others similar not shown.

D-37. Well-made black flint drill with one spatulate end. L: 57 mm - w: 11 mm. Maximum thickness 7 mm. Figure 17, *w*; Plate X, *w*.

D-75. A tiny drill, shaped more or less like the projectile points and, like them, basally edge ground. It is finely flaked toward the point. L: 19 mm. Thickness 3 mm. Probably longer originally.

The series of gravers (Figure 18, *a-f*) are all of tan or grey chert. D-96 (Figure 18, *d*) has two worked points. Other gravers have been found on the surface in the general area.

Figures D-9 (Figure 17, *e*; Plate X, *e*) 10 (Figure 17, *c*; Plate X, *c*) and 48 (Figure 17, *d*; Plate X, *d*) are portions of well-made knives or blanks with some edge chipping. D-16 (Figure 17, *b*; Plate X, *b*) is an ovoid knife of fine workmanship, picked up on the surface a few yards east of the site, just before the sand was removed from there and before an early site was suspected. It has characteristic flat flaking and is made of dark, mottled flint similar to some of the site material.

Two gritty sandstone abraders worn concave on one face were recovered from there. A 3 1/2-inch chert preform was found later beneath the deep sand at the east end of the site.

Illustrated on the following page, fragments P (Figure 18, *i*) and P-1 (Figure 18, *j*) point ends of fluted, heavy spears, and a base tang, are surface finds from a field just east of the site discussed below. The typical Holcombe fluted blade P-2 (Figure 18, *k*) is from the surface of a nearby farm at the same 610-foot elevation. The single flute is 33 mm long. It has edge grinding.

A (Figure 18, *g*) and A-1 (Figure 18, *h*) are local "Plano" types, usually considered more recent than fluted blades. B (Figure 18, *i*) is the basal end of a local Scottsbluff (Satchell) type of fine workmanship. Both A and B were found well below the 600-foot level in Chesterfield Township, Macomb County, Michigan, and Sandwich West in Essex County, Ontario, Canada, respectively. A-1 is a common local point similar to the "Hi-Lo" points of western Michigan. All are basally ground.

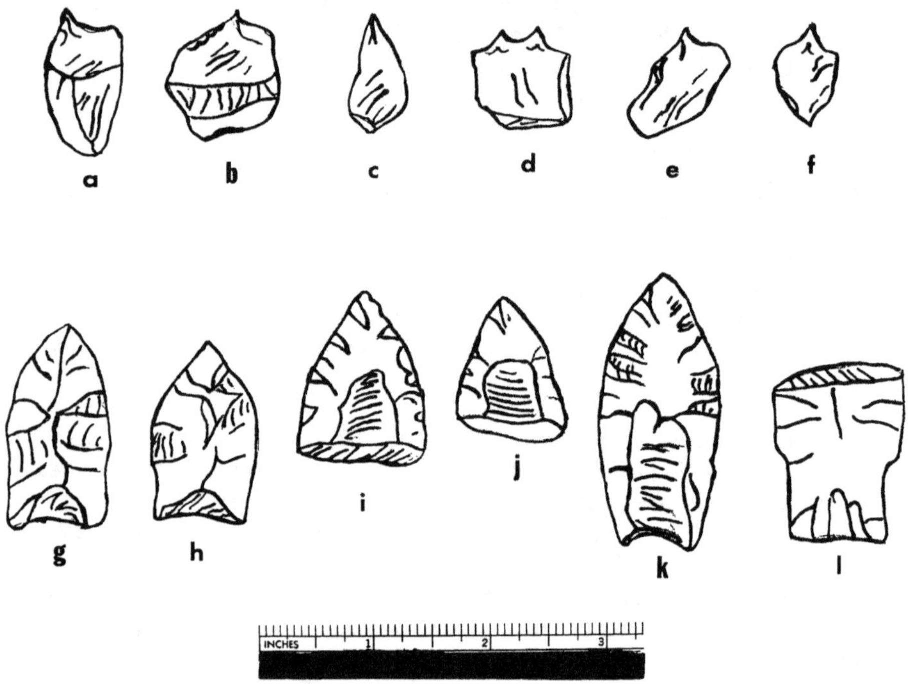


FIG. 18. Artifacts from Paleo-II and other areas in Macomb County: *a-f*, gravers; *g-h*, aquaplano points; *i-j*, tips of large fluted points; *k*, point similar to those from the Holcombe site; *l*, Scottsbluff-like point base.

## Comments and Discussion

Some varieties of flint and chert used on the site of Paleo-II do not seem to be of local origin. An examination of Ohio fluited points gives the impression that some of this material is similar. This applies especially to certain dark bluish-mottled and some black flint (base 122), probably Upper Mercer. Some of the material used is of poorer quality, probably local.

Channel flakes have been found which seem to indicate that in the case of multiple fluting the central flakes were removed first. The samples illustrated still show the original cross flaking of the blade along the outer margins; but such flake scars had already been obliterated from one margin by the previous removal of a channel flake. This observation is not possible from a study of the finished point alone.

In some instances hinge fractures terminate fluting before it is well started. On the other hand, D-35 is channeled about half its length. D-32 is not fluted at all, nor is it basally ground, as is almost universal in completed points. Since the basal thickness of this point is only 3.5 mm perhaps fluting was impractical or at least unnecessary. Fluting is functional and only enough is necessary to serve its purpose. Points gradually tapered to a thin base would fit the shaft cleft with little or no fluting, which would only weaken thin basal ends. Some of the base stubs are fluted only on one side while others have channels that extend beyond the fracture on one or both faces. Channels are either single or made by striking off several small flakes, usually three. Base 122 was found in two pieces. Fluting runs more than 30 mm, and on one face, beyond the break. Fluting is always necessarily shallow.

There is a tendency to classify these points as unfluted and to describe them as "basally thinned" only. Basal thinning is a rather ambiguous term, especially applicable to square-based types like Milnesand which has a row of flakes removed all the way across the base. Our points are centrally thinned by fluting strokes that create a concavity, as is also the case with Clovis points. Even where the flutes are very short and incipient, it is still often apparent that fluting was attempted but hinged off short. In addition, every base has edge grinding and a few are ground between the tangs also. Grinding is not present in points D-9 and D-30 which were probably defective.

The extent of channeling may have been limited by some rather poor quality material used; or in other cases because of the deliberate, gradual thinning of the points towards the base. Only 3 or 4 mm of stock remain in some specimens. Most other Michigan fluted points studied are rather thick and depend upon the flute to thin them enough for streamlined hafting. Among Mason's illustrations of Michigan fluted points only 2 or 3 from

Lapeer and Washtenaw counties are typically Holcombe. Recently two have been reported from near Grand Rapids and two were found on old 610 by 15-foot beaches in Wayne and Monroe counties (Weir and Grogitsky collections); and a few similar points are reported from Northern Ohio (Prufer, 1964). Once seen, these spearheads are readily identified. The better examples of Holcombe points, like P-2 and D-53 are far superior in technique of workmanship to many Michigan fluted points. The delicacy and flatness of the flake scars are remarkable. The "pumpkin seed" type from Paleo-II is unusual for Michigan and seems to resemble the wide, "bilaterally symmetrical ovoid blades" discussed by Mason and found principally in the Delaware Valley. The straight or parallel-sided point seems to be lacking on Paleo-II.

The contention that Holcombe points are not really fluted and not typologically related to Clovis, being rather a later Plano transitional type is, perhaps, justified by some characteristics. These would include: (*a*) thinness with flat flake-scars and lack of edge retouching, in contrast to heavy deep-fluted, edge-trimmed types; (*b*) the scarcity of long channeling and the occasional lack of it; and (*c*) the occurrence of some small points considered unsuited to big game hunting; (*d*) the supposed recency of Holcombe points as compared to those more typically Clovis forms.

That these differences are not entirely conclusive is apparent. A lack of long channel scars, or even their occasional absence, is not alone a deciding factor. Wormington (1957: 34) reports a number of thin, unfluted points intermixed with classic Folsoms at the Lindenmier site (10,800 B.P.). These were called "Midland" although actually made by the "Folsom" hunters themselves. The same was true for the Scharbauer, Texas, site where unfluted Clovis types found with the fluted points were reported to be the thin specimens. Few Clovis points have extensive fluting, which is really a Folsom trait. Neither is size a determining factor, although it is true that points seem to be larger in the western than in parts of the eastern United States. Small short points were found, however, at the Lehner mammoth kill mixed with long, classic Clovis points. Apparently the Paleo-Indian used all of his flake blanks, whether large or small. Fluting on one face only is also of common occurrence elsewhere, a Clovis trait.

Holcombe could possibly be transitional between accepted Clovis types and such thick, always unfluted, Plano lanceolates with concave bases, as are plentiful here and elsewhere, but it is hard to imagine a transition to such stemmed points as

Scottsbluff or early side-notched points with straight-based bottoms. More logically, these would develop from comparatively square-bottomed points like Milnesand or Plainview. The persistence of incipient fluting with resulting basal concavity, beyond the appearance of square stems like Scottsbluff, has not been demonstrated, and it is still not certain that a traceable straight-line evolution of points ever actually took place. Overlapping and borrowing occurred, of course, but stemmed points were present in certain cultural areas as far back as 9,000 years ago.

We also find considerable difficulty in attempting to segregate Holcombe points from the more standard fluted types on a time basis, although Clovis is admittedly a very ancient form. On the same beach, same 610 foot elevation, and only a short distance east of Paleo-II, two fragmentary blades and a heavy tang have recently been found, possibly representing another, yet unlocated, Early Man site. These are illustrated as P (Figure 18, *i*) and P-1 (Figure 18, *j*). They are typically heavy, fluted points with channels extending well up towards the point end. P has long flute scars on both faces as shown. P-1 has typical Clovis type edge trimming in addition. P-2 is a very fine, thin example of the Holcombe type. It was found on a nearby field at the same elevation. Thickness within the flute of the heavy type is 6 mm, or equal to the maximum over-all thickness of Holcombe points. Note that the points described all come from the same Lake Clinton beach. If all these points are not "Clovis type," then we cannot recognize such by sight. They certainly are not typical Plano types.

The Scottsbluff type and some local Plano points have been found at lower levels, suggesting that these are more recent than Holcombe. A few bases of the Holcombe type have pronounced edge grinding, suggesting to some that the Scottsbluff shoulder is a development of this practice. None of the specimens from Paleo-II are so heavily ground and there is no hint of a shoulder. None of the thirty local Scottsbluff (or Satchell) bases examined has any edge grinding.

If Holcombe is in the Plano or Aquaplano tradition, and an evolutionary stage in the development of archaic points, then considerable time will have to be found for these changes. We can not reasonably crowd a multiplicity of later Plano types between Holcombe and earliest archaic in the space of a few hundred years. Even late point styles lasted a long time.

It would seem that we are tentatively justified in estimating a date of about 9,000 years B. C. for the Paleo-II occupation.

Any fluted points deposited then (or later) might well be found in the whole lower Michigan peninsula. For some reason none have appeared above the Port Huron moraine system.

The question often arises, "Did the site occupants hunt the mastodon or mammoth?" We have no "recent" mammoth dates, but the woody contents of the Tupperville, Ontario, mastodon skull, found near Lake St. Clair, yielded an age of about 6,300 years. A similar reading was obtained from a Michigan mastodon tusk. Critics are of the opinion that the materials used for dating were not suitable for reliable testing and that the date is much too recent. Many biologists believe that the mastodon survived until about 8,500 years ago. If we accept either opinion, the site occupants could have hunted them. We have no evidence that they actually did. At Paleo-II we found no skeletal remains, no fireplaces, and not even stones large enough to break up marrow bones. The thin covering of beach sand did not help to preserve perishable material on this site, open to thousands of years of frost, rain, and weather. Hunters of large herd animals probably consumed heavy quarry at the site of the kill. Direct evidence that our paleo-hunters pursued the mastodon will have to come from such a site.

Previous studies had suggested that Lake Algonquin existed 9,000 years ago. In accordance with the revision worked out by J. L. Hough, employing the latest datings and information of Broecker and Farrand, the interval should be considered as beginning well before 12,000 B.P. and lasting until about 11,000 B.P. The aquaplano tradition, following true fluted points, must according to this reckoning also be pushed back more than 1,000 years.

We feel that Holcombe points preceed the Aquaplano types and consequently should be dated to at least 9,000 B. C. This also provides the time needed for the development or introduction of very early Archaic point types.

# VI

## PALEO-II-W: A MINOR PALEO-INDIAN OCCUPATION SITE

In March, 1963, Jerry DeVisscher recognized another small but interesting Paleo-hunters' occupation site from the characteristic thin, tiny, secondary flakes that appeared on the surface after a very heavy rain. It was located only 440 feet west of DeVisscher Paleo-II site. Like the DeVisscher site it was situated in the southwest quarter of the southwest quarter of section 23, Sterling Township, Macomb County. The elevation of this sand ridge, which seems to overlie a clay drumlin, is 610 feet above sea level. The ridge varies in elevation from 609 feet to 614 feet and was a bar or sandy beach of glacial Lake Clinton. The site has been under cultivation for generations and a general eastward drifting of the sandy surface has taken place forming small dunes and altering original surface levels, thus eliminating possible stratigraphic features. We have designated the site Paleo-II-W.

The heaviest occurrence of flakes and artifacts was confined to an area roughly circular and 35 feet in diameter with occasional finds immediately outside this concentration. DeVisscher, assisted by some members of the Aboriginal Research Club of Detroit, recovered artifacts of the "paleo" tradition with no pottery or Woodland artifacts within the area of concentration. The finds, the majority of which came from the plow zone, consisted of broken basal ends of lanceolate points, one entire point, distal ends, gravers, a spokeshave scraper, one blank, knives, abraders, side and end scrapers and several nondescript, slightly flaked or used spalls. Numerous thin, secondary flakes were in evidence everywhere but very few rough, thick spalls were found. We consider this to be evidence that the artifacts from this site were also made almost entirely from preformed blanks, probably brought from some distance. Even the rough scrapers could have been made from broken blanks, although this is not certain.

Typologically, the artifacts are similar to those from nearby Paleo-II. Some basal sections bear enough similarity to suggest manufacture by the same craftsmen. The artifacts also resemble those from the Holcombe site one-half mile west which was excavated by the University of Michigan. There is one more-or-less parallel-sided, round-end portion (Figure 19, 6; Plate XI, 6) fluted to within 4 mm of the point which differs from the other points. This closely resembles the Folsom type or possibly the Barnes points from Saginaw County (Roosa, 1963).

Figure 19, *a*; (Plate XI, *a*) shows both faces of the only whole point recovered. It is thin with extensive fluting on one face. The reverse face has collateral flaking but only a short basal flute. It was found 10 inches below the surface and perhaps had been discarded after a fluting stroke carried away a small portion of the base and one tang. It is smoothly ground. Examination of other Holcombe points, as these thin, characteristic points have come to be known, indicates that the best cross flaking is almost always found on the flatter of the asymmetrical, lenticular faces. Finished Holcombe points and sections are smoothly lenticular in cross section with one face more convex than the other. The longest and best channeling is done on the more convex face.

Figure 19, *c* (Plate XI, *c*) is an unfluted lanceolate with the point and part of the base missing. It is made of exotic, translucent chalcedony which is purple-grey in color with flecks of tan and orange. This seems to be the only paleo-point of similar material so far reported from the state. It is quite thin and the lower edges are ground.

Figure 19, *d* (Plate XI, *d*) is a point end of greyish chert. It came from the surface just outside the area of concentration. It has collateral flaking. The question of how far such small objects can be transported by land cultivation will be discussed later. Figure 19, *e* (Plate XI, *e*) is a large flint distal end section of good workmanship.

Figure 19, *f*-*m* (Plate XI, *f*-*m*) are the basal sections of fluted and incipiently fluted lanceolate points (see table for measurements). Of the nine bases two are black with a little mottling, as was one large, crude scraper. This is a minority material on local Early Man sites. Most artifacts are made of light-colored chert. The presence of a large number of bases as compared to the few distal ends, indicates that the spear shafts of the hunting occupants of the site were rearmed with new points here also. The basal fragments that remained attached to the foreshaft were removed and discarded. Ends from the broken points of the spearheads probably remained in the game, which often escaped if only slightly wounded. Note the rather consistent three mm thickness in the fluted area.

Figure 19, *n*-*t* (Plate XI, *n*-*t*) are gravers. Five of these are

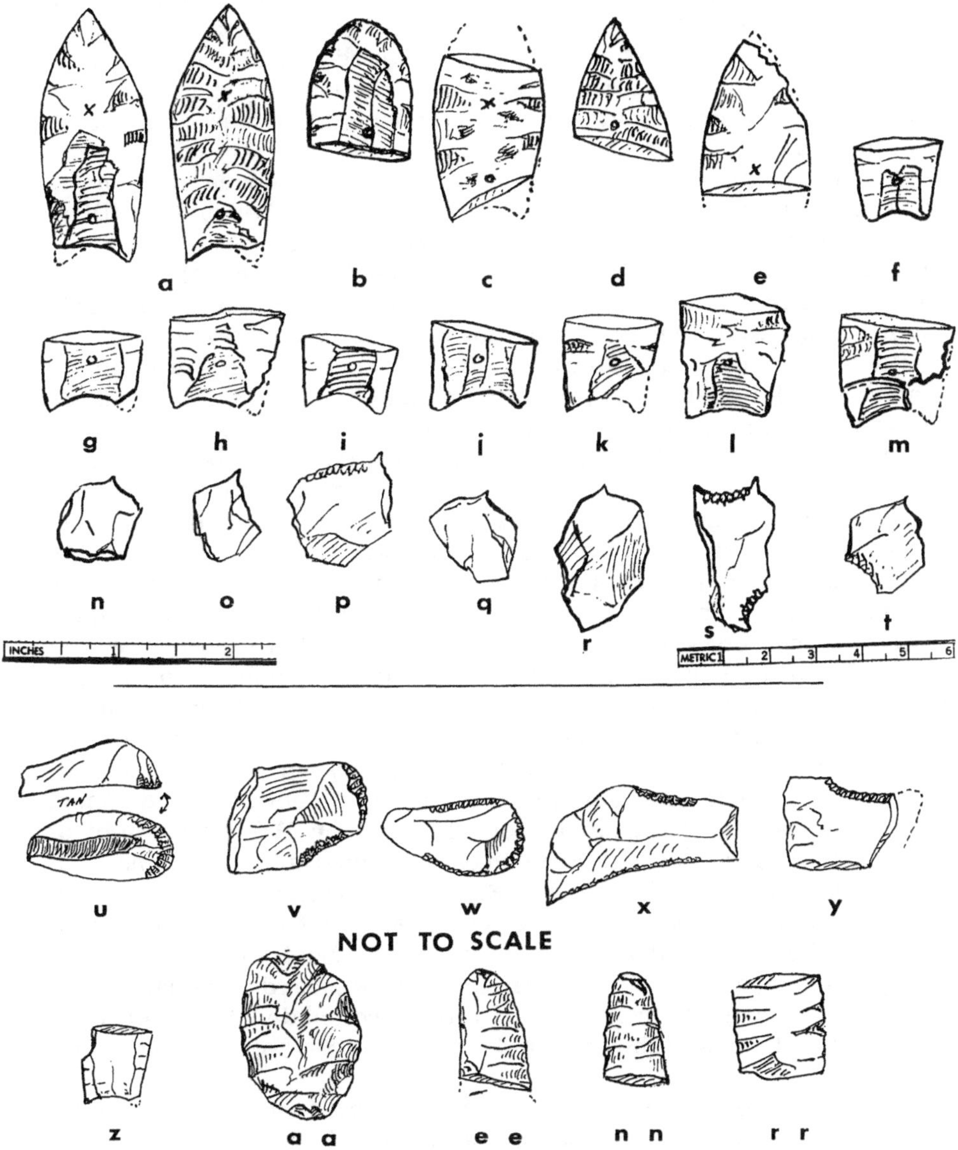


FIG. 19. Artifacts from Paleo-II-W: *a*, projectile point; *b-e*, point tips and fragments; *f-m*, point bases; *n-t*, gravers; *u-y*, scrapers; *z*, point base; *aa*, preform; *ee*, *nn*, convergent biface tips; *rr*, medial fragment.

thin, conventional, single-point tools. Some of the spurs are dulled. One graver (Figure 19, *p*; Plate XI, *p*) is a combination tool with a finely chipped scraping edge adjacent to the spur. Figure 19, *s* (Plate XI, *s*) is double pointed, with fine, regular flaking between the spurs. Another worked area occurs at the opposite end which is also pointed and could be tne remains of another spur.

Gravers are thought to be indicative of a bone- or ivory-working culture. They seem to function best when used with a gouging motion to create either linear designs or to excavate pits or perhaps to gouge eyeholes in needles, such as have been found in European Upper Paleolithic tool assemblages. Experiment shows that the spur will cut thin skins very well. They could have served as tatooing points if that practice was in vogue among the Paleo-hunters, but this would not account for the wear on some of them. On this site no scrap of wood or osseous material survived, so local graver function can only be surmised.

Figure 19, *v-y* (Plate XI, *v, w, x*) shows an interesting series of scrapers. Figure 19, *v* and *w*, are end scrapers of the steep-bit variety which are often associated with ancient cultures. An additional end scraper, a flatter form, was found in two pieces, 23 feet apart. The fact that the working section was sheared off suggests that considerable force accompanied its use. It was probably broken while being used on wood or bone. No stone tools other than flaked flints were used by Paleolithic people in their carpentry. The spokeshave scraper, Figure 19, *y*, is an outstanding example of an ancient woodworking tool. It, like its modern facsimile, is adapted to forming, smoothing, and tapering round shafts. It is diagnostic of very old or Paleolithic tool assemblages. One end had been broken from this specimen.

Figure 19, *v* and *x* (Plate XI, *x*) are general-purpose scrapers and side scrapers. Figure 19, *x* seems to have had a graving spur but it is difficult to be positive about this. Steep end scrapers are almost always made of good, hard flint but some of the thinner, cruder, nondescript tools are made of poorer cherts. These would be suitable for hide scraping or work on soft materials.

Large, ovoid, uniface knives have been found on this ridge and one such was attributed to the Paleo-II site. We did not find any of this type on Paleo-II-W. The only well-made tool that would serve efficiently as a knife is Figure 19, *ee* (Plate XI,*nn*), with additional segment found after the drawing was made). It was formed on a flat, unifacial spall and was well-flaked and sharp. Rounded off points like Figure 19, *b* (Plate XI, *b*) probably also served as knives. Figure 19, *aa*; (Plate XI, *aa*) is a small blank of material common to the site. Another, similar blank of black flint is not illustrated. A blank of chert from Paleo-II site was more elongated.

A number of miscellaneous thin, sharp spalls, some of them slightly worked or edge-fractured by use were recovered. One had a section of very fine micro-flaking along one edge. Experiment indicates that these are ideally suited to cutting new meat. A few additional nondescript spalls were also found but not illustrated. A flat abrader of fine, gritty sandstone, and some worn pebbles of the same material were also unearthed.

Early the following spring, it was possible to do some digging around the periphery of the site. We were rewarded with a few artifact fragments, some of which are quite interesting. Figure 18, *z* is the mottled, light-grey basal half of a fluted lanceolate point. One tang is missing. Two broken basal sections were found, the first dark grey, the other mottled brown chert. Figure 19, *rr* is the midsection of a large point, light tan in color, stained with rusty spots. Figure 19, *nn* is a tan chert knife or end tool section made of a spall, but worked on both sides. Note the transversal flaking. We also found a glossy black channel flake, apparently a widening flake, as a previous channel is visible on its right. All of the specimens are thin, typically Holcombe in character with shallow, flat flaking.

The finding of artifacts well outside the main concentration of a cultivated campsite may be due either to transportation by farm implements or by having been thrown or carried from the work area by the original occupants. The fact that land is plowed and that wind blows from different directions at different times tends to prevent these activities from transporting objects very far from their original locations. The location of crockery sherds which we deposited in a cultivated field experimentally several seasons ago seems to substantiate this.

The digging of a paleo-site always gives rise to the hope that some notable feature of occupation will appear in the subsoil. At Paleo-II-W, circular molds and dark streaks usually proved to be rodent burrows or deep plow scars. Only two faint molds, about 8 inches in diameter, were found that did not exhibit the characteristics of filled-in burrows. They were 13 feet apart and extended straight into the subsoils for 7 or 8 inches below the plow zone. No other similar features were identified. This could be due to the fact that they had been obliterated by the numerous old burrows that crisscross the sandy soil. There was no evidence of firepits even though no occupation site is without one or more. Such features must have been obliterated by thousands of years of exposure to frost, rain, and flood. It is entirely possible that storm flooding covered the site in Lake Nipissing times, some 4,200 years ago, when water levels again attained the 605 foot level. At any rate, only lithic material remains.

The probable age of the Paleo-II-W occupation must be similar to that proposed for DeVisscher Paleo-II and Holcombe: that is, at least 11,000 years old. This estimate is based on the date attributed to the Lake Clinton beaches upon which these sites are situated. This estimate will remain valid as long as points are not found much below the 605-foot level. At that time, all lower land surfaces were under water. Up to the present none have been reported from such lower levels despite aroused interest in Paleo-sites in this general area where much of the land lies below 600 feet. Of the ancient point types, only Hi-Lo, Satchell (Scottsbluff), archaic side-notched points with ground bases, and one thick lanceolate "aquaplano" point have been attributed to sites below the 600-foot level.

The sand ridge upon which Paleo-II-W is situated continues

TABLE 39

TABLE OF MEASUREMENTS

(All Measurements in Millimeters)

| Illustration | | Maximum Length | Maximum Width | Basal Width | Length of Obverse Flute | Length of Reverse Flute | Max. Thickness | Thickness in Flute |
|---|---|---|---|---|---|---|---|---|
| Figure 19 | Plate XI | | | | | | | |
| *a* | *a* | 55 | 22 | 15 | 19 | 10 | 4 | 2 |
| *b* | *b* | 28 | 21 | 24 | .. | .. | .. | 2 |
| *c* | *c* | 33 | 25 | .. | .. | .. | 3 | 4 |
| *d* | *d* | 28 | 22 | .. | .. | .. | 5 | .. |
| *e* | *e* | 35 | 24 | .. | .. | .. | 5 | .. |
| *f* | *f* | .. | .. | 13 | 8 | 8 | .. | 3 |
| *g* | *g* | .. | .. | 18 | 6 | 6+ | .. | 3 |
| *h* | *h* | .. | .. | 18 | 14 | .. | .. | 3 |
| *i* | *i* | .. | .. | 16 | 16+ | 16+ | .. | 3 |
| *j* | *j* | .. | .. | 19 | 19+ | .. | .. | .. |
| *k* | *k* | .. | .. | 16 | 9 | 6 | .. | 3 |
| *l* | *l* | 26 | .. | 14 | 12 | .. | .. | .. |
| *m* | *m* | 28 | 28 | 19 | .. | .. | .. | 4 |

about one mile farther to the east and aboriginal sites of all ages are found on it. Some well-fluted, sometimes heavy, lanceolate spear fragments found in two locations on this ancient beach are of interest to this discussion. These seem to be much more extensively fluted than Holcombe, both in length and depth of flute channel. In this same general area extremely large, basally ground Hi-Lo point sections have been found, in addition to stray Holcombe points. The high, sandy beach was a favored thoroughfare through low-lying, swampy terrain, and it was a suitable habitation site for people from Paleo-Indian times to Late Woodland times. Subsequently, the white settler sought out these high, dry ridges in pioneer days. A log house once stood near this site.

## VII

### PALEO-II-W-A: THE FOURTH MACOMB COUNTY PALEO-OCCUPATION SITE

This Paleo-hunter site, the fourth found by Jerry DeVisscher of Mount Clemens on the same sand ridge, was located only about 100 feet from the site reported as Paleo-II-W. It was thought to be a possible extention of the latter, so the letter A was merely added to differentiate the occupation areas. This site was also discovered after minute examination of the surface revealed characteristic, tiny secondary flakes left by the site's occupants. Two concentrations were evident some 20 feet apart, possibly indicating the location of two work or shelter sites closely adjacent to one another.

One hundred thirty-one five-foot squares were excavated, mostly by DeVisscher himself in spare time. Digging was also done by Edward J. Wahla of Roseville, and one "community dig" was conducted in September, 1964, when the site was in imminent danger of destruction by subdivision development.

The top soil disturbed by the plow to a depth of 8 inches, was run through the portable, gasoline-powered sifter with interchangeable screens, as with the two previous sites. The subsoil was troweled and scraped down to sterile sand which lay from 12 to 17 inches beneath the surface. The "community dig" was conducted by fifteen members of the Michigan Archaeological Society and the Aboriginal Research Club of Detroit. This work produced three artifacts in a square dug by Paul Laut—one end scraper, a fluted basal stub, and a point tang found at the south edge of the site. A very fine large, distal section of a Holcombe point was later uncovered by excavating machinery just east of the site beneath four feet of duned sterile sand, and three additional point ends were excavated near by, just before the site was destroyed.

Careful watch was kept for features, especially for ash pits, which might contain bone fragments as was the case on the Holcombe site. No such features were found, however, and nothing but lithic material was encountered.

Two excellent, small LeCroy bifurcate-stemmed points and a

damaged, corner-notched projectile point were sifted out of the surface sand from the plow zone. No potsherds were found.

The site had evidently been the location of a nineteenth-century dwelling. The yield of dozens of square nails, broken glass, crockery sherds, buttons, lumps of plaster and 9 Indian head pennies (1872-1884) lent variety but did not make the work easier.

Paleo-II-W-A differed from the other sites on the ridge only in the proportionate number of certain artifact types, and in the smaller amount of flakes and rejectage encountered. Out of a total "finished" tool assemblage of 56 pieces, 18 were well-made scrapers; but no true "spokeshave" was found on the site. The proportion of whole or slightly damaged projectile points was also higher in proportion to the basal sections found, about 1:1. There were 10 rather large sections and 3 additional point tips. There were 10 bases, none belonging with the distal ends found.

The largest fluted point fragment (Catalog number 371) was perhaps originally 6.6 cm long or longer. It was manufactured of bluish-grey mottled chert, and was extensively fluted on both faces. It has a maximum thickness of only 5 mm, with 3 mm in the fluted area.

The basal portion, Number 377 (Figure 20, *k*; Plate XII, *k*), could have been from a equally large specimen. It, too, is extensively fluted, 30 mm of channeling still remaining below the break. It is laterally ground, as is 371.

The occurrence of these large specimens seems to indicate that much of the Holcombe point population consisted of larger spears than is indicated by the average run of points remaining on the occupation sites here. Also, comparison of the poor quality of most projectile points recovered in the excavations with the fine quality of most of the distal ends (like numbers 440 and 220, probably recovered from game killed) makes it clear that most of the tools found on the sites are rejects or damaged specimens. The Paleo-hunter seldom lost any of his fine spears due to carelessness about the camp.

Note that on Number 434 (Figure 20, *a*; Plate XII, *a*) which is part of a large, unifacially fluted point, a graving spur had been made by the removal of a few flakes at the edge of the original fracture. This shows evidence of having been a carefully executed job, not an accidental occurrence.

Artifacts 171, 269, and 341 are probably knives or knife sections. Artifact Number 261 is unifacially worked.

Artifact 290 (Figure 20, *d*; Plate XII, *d*) and 365 (Figure 20, *e*; Plate XII, *e*) are virtually completed points. The short, wide

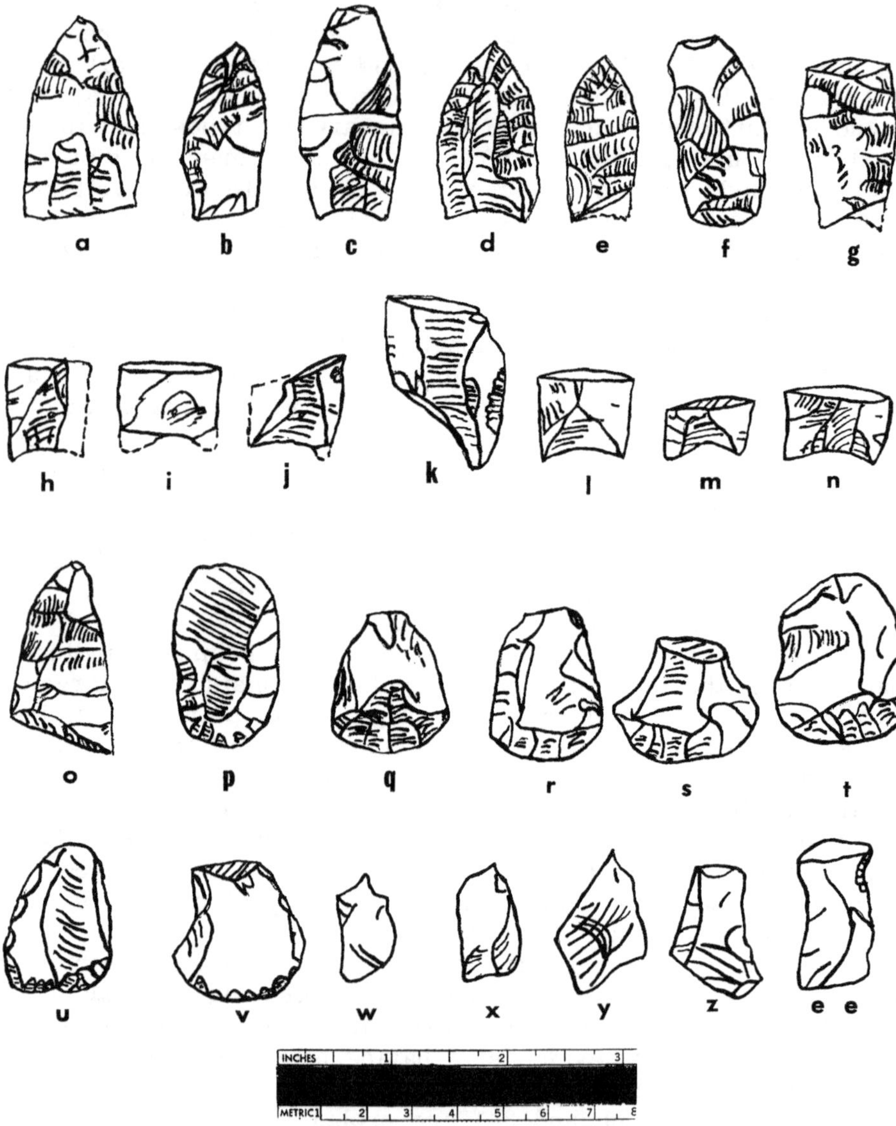


FIG. 20. Artifacts from Paleo-II-W-A: *a-g*, points and point fragments; *h-n*, point bases; *o*, convergent biface tip; *p-v*, scrapers; *w-y*, gravers; *z*, *ee*, utilized flakes.

specimen is well fluted on one face, has lateral grinding and is made of grey chert stained tan as is quite common with light-colored stone here. Artifact 365 is remarkable in that it is the smallest, well-made Holcombe point recovered. It is only 34 mm long, 16 mm wide, and 3 mm in maximum thickness. It has 4 mm of basal thinning and is edge ground, indicating that it was a functional point. It is collaterally flaked. It was discarded because of a damaged base. It would be interesting to know whether such small points were intended for some specialized use (some suggest wildfowl hunting) or whether they are only the result of the economical use of the available flint.

Specimens 302 (Figure 20, *b*; Plate XII, *b*) and 386 (Figure 20, *g*; Plate XII, *g*) are somewhat constricted toward the base; however, the stem-like shape of number 302 is largely due to accidental lateral fracture along one lower edge. Specimen number 301 (Figure 20, *c*; Plate XII, *c*) was recovered from two different squares. Its original length was a little more than two inches.

Artifact number 270 is a good quality projectile tip and 440 is a larger distal end of excellent workmanship with shallow, delicate flaking. There are remains of lateral grinding near the point of fracture. It is an example of the very sharp, pointed tip-end found in most of the better Holcombe spears.

Figure 20, *h-n* (Plate XII, *h-n*) illustrates some of the ten bases of projectile points recovered from this site. A few fragments are rather small but all are laterally ground and three are also basally ground. The thickness of the material left in the center of the fluted area averages 3 mm, which was also the case with points from the other sites considered here.

The largest section, number 377 (Figure 20, *k*; Plate XII, *k*) was certainly part of a good-sized spear, apparently very extensively fluted. All bases are of light-colored chert, often with traces of rusty discoloration or patina. Most of the artifacts found are made of Bayport Chert, a native Michigan product.

The scrapers shown in Figure 20, *p-v* (Plate XII, *p-v*) are all manufactured on chert spalls or cores except specimen 312 (Figure 20, *s*; Plate XII, *s*). Not only is this made of glossy, black flint, but it is also equipped with two Paleo-type graving spurs, one at each angle where the tool widens into the bit.

The end scrapers, 363 (Figure 20, *g*; Plate XII, *g*), 369 (Figure 20, *r*; Plate XII, *r*), 412 (Figure 20, *b*; Plate XII, *b*), 422 (Figure 20, *v*; Plate XII, *v*), are well-made, steep-bitted tools and rather uniform in size. Specimen 331 (not illustrated) and 332 (Figure 20, *r*; Plate XII, *r*) are larger side scrapers, unifacially worked as are the others in this series. Small thumb scrapers like 357 and 369 (not illustrated) are not as carefully made. In fact, a large number of crude tools made on flakes were recovered from the site. Some of the better of these are shown as specimens 316 (Figure 20, *z*; Plate XII, *z*), 364 (Figure 20, *ee*; Plate XII, *ee*), and 415. More than 60 such artifacts show some minor alteration or marks of use. Many of them may well have served as knives, judging from their thinness and keen edges.

Figure 20, *w-y*, shows three of five gravers from the site. Three of them are made on small, flat spalls but numbers 314 and 382 are rather exceptional tools. Artifact number 382 is a carefully made multiple-spurred graver, manufactured on what was once a Holcombe projectile point. It is very symmetrical, bifacially worked, and has some retouch along one edge. The three graving spurs occupy the normal positions of the three natural points or angles of the original tool, one being worked on the tip, and two near former basal corners. The graver is (now) 42 mm in length and the material is a good grade of mottled, dark gray chert.

In addition to the artifacts described, two fragmentary preforms or blanks were excavated (numbers 319, 392). A small, well-worn sandstone abrader was also found beneath the plow zone.

Paleo-II-W-A apparently was a single component, Paleo-occupation site with only three "strays" or later artifacts recovered—all surface finds. This is about par for the 3300 square feet excavated judging from the amount of similar intrusive material scattered over this long-popular sand ridge.

The statement made in earlier reports regarding the occurrence of Holcombe points only on terrain lying above 605 feet is still valid. Despite accelerated archaeological activity in this area no such points have been found below that level, although a considerable number of so-called Plano or very late Paleo-Indian or transitional projectiles have been reported, such as Hi-Lo and Satchell points.

TABLE 40

TABLE OF METRIC DIMENSIONS OF ARTIFACTS AS NUMBERED IN ACCOMPANYING DRAWINGS

| Catalog Number | Length (mm) | Maximum Width (mm) | Width at Base (mm) | Maximum Thickness (mm) | Thickness at Base (mm) | Fluting (mm) |
|---|---|---|---|---|---|---|
| 371 | 53 | 26 | 22 | 5 | 3 | . . . |
| 409 | 42 | 25 | 25 | 5 | 4 | obverse 16<br>reverse . . |
| 269 | 41 | 23 | . . . | 4 | . . . | . . . |
| 366 | 38 | 20 | . . . | 4 | . . . | . . . |
| 171 | 33 | 17 | . . . | 5 | . . . | . . . |
| 302 | 41 | 19 | 14 | 4.5 | 2 | . . . |
| 301 | 46 | 21 | 15 | 7 | 3 | . . . |
| 386 | 37 | 22 | 15 | 5.5 | 3 | . . . |
| 290 | 39 | 22 | 20 | 4 | 3 | obverse 29<br>reverse 5 |
| 365 | 34 | 16 | 14 | 3.5 | 1.5 | obverse 4<br>reverse . . |
| 270 | 30 | . . . | . . . | . . . | 4 | . . . |
| 341 | 36 | . . . | . . . | . . . | 4 | . . . |
| 334 | 43 | 25 | 23 | . . . | 5 | . . . |
| 382 | 42 | 19 | . . . | . . . | 5 | . . . |

PART III

# THE PALEO-INDIAN OCCUPATION OF THE HOLCOMBE BEACH

*James E. Fitting*

## VIII

## SITE COMPARISONS

### The DeVisscher Collections

In the spring of 1965 DeVisscher made available, for study and comparison, his collection of chippage from all four localities along the Holcombe beach. In addition to all of the débitage recovered from Paleo-II, Paleo-II-W, and Paleo-II-W-A, this collection included 3,418 chert fragments from the Holcombe site itself. These were excavated by DeVisscher after the University of Michigan field party left the site in 1961. He had been sending the artifacts recovered from the Holcombe site to the Museum as he found them.

DeVisscher had been working in the area to the south of Area I at the Holcombe site where he screened a number of 5-foot squares. Before including this material with the previously studied Holcombe sample for intersite comparisons, it was necessary to compare it with other samples from the site. A comparison of percentages of flake types is given in Table 41. It would seem that this additional material differed from both of the other samples.

A more valid comparison, however, would be with the flake-type groups noted in the collections from the excavations. This comparison is given in Table 42. It is apparent that this additional DeVisscher material belongs with Flake Group III, the group containing the highest numbers of retouch flakes. This is exactly the flake group which we would expect in the area directly to the south of Area I if we are to complete the symmetry of the camp. This additional material from DeVisscher's excavations represents one or more of the finishing or family areas of

TABLE 41

PERCENTAGES OF FLAKE TYPES

Percentages of Flake Types in the University of Michigan Museum of Anthropology Excavated Sample, the DeVisscher Surface Collection, and the DeVisscher Excavations at the Holcombe Site. This Represents the Total Sample of Chippage from the Holcombe Site.

| | UMMA Excavation | | DeVisscher Surface Collection | | DeVisscher Excavation | |
|---|---|---|---|---|---|---|
| | N | Per Cent | N | Per Cent | N | Per Cent |
| Flakes with striking platforms . . | 90 | 2 | 126 | 5 | 51 | 1 |
| Flakes without striking platforms . . . . . . . . . . . . . . . | 215 | 4 | 69 | 3 | 53 | 2 |
| Block fracture flakes . . . . . . . . | 721 | 14 | 360 | 14 | 223 | 7 |
| Small retouch flakes . . . . . . . . . | 4117 | 80 | 1952 | 78 | 3099 | 90 |
| Total . . . . . . . . . . . . . . . . | 5143 | | 2517 | | 3418 | |

TABLE 42

FLAKES AND FLAKE GROUPS FROM THE HOLCOMBE SITE

Percentages of Flake Types from the DeVisscher Excavations at the Holcombe Site Compared with the Flake Groups Established in the Area of the University of Michigan Excavations at the Site

| | Flakes with Striking Platforms | Flakes without Striking Platforms | Block Fracture Flakes | Small Retouch Flakes |
|---|---|---|---|---|
| N. . . . . . . . . . | 51 | 53 | 223 | 3099 |
| Per Cent . . . . | 1 | 2 | 7 | 90 |
| Chert Groups All Per Cent | | | | |
| Group I. . . . . | 1 | 4 | 44 | 51 |
| Group II . . . . | 2 | 4 | 27 | 67 |
| Group III. . . . | 1 | 2 | 3 | 94 |
| Group IV. . . . | 3 | 5 | 13 | 79 |

the site and can be opposed to the central area represented by Flake Groups I and, to a lesser extent, II.

An examination of the percentages of chert types among the chippage and comparisons with the chert groups established earlier (Table 43) indicates a near identity to Chert Group III. This is the chert group represented in the southwest of Area I and northeast of Area II. Again, it is the chert group which might be predicted for the area where DeVisscher excavated.

The additional DeVisscher collection fits well within the framework of chert and flake-type distribution on the site and can be added to the original Holcombe sample with no problems. Indeed, since it completes the symmetry of the site our sample is more valid with it than without it.

TABLE 43

CHERT AND CHERT GROUPS FROM THE HOLCOMBE SITE

Percentages of Chert Types From the DeVisscher Excavations at the Holcombe Site Compared with Chert Groups Established in the University of Michigan Excavations at the Site

| | White Bayport | Light Grey Bayport | Dark Grey Bayport | Exotic |
|---|---|---|---|---|
| N. . . . . . . . . . . . . . . | 828 | 1759 | 704 | 127 |
| Per Cent . . . . . . . . . | 24 | 51 | 21 | 4 |
| Chert Group (Per Cent) | | | | |
| Group I. . . . . . . . . . | 28 | 27 | 23 | 22 |
| Group II . . . . . . . . . | 17 | 52 | 29 | 2 |
| Group III. . . . . . . . . | 24 | 53 | 19 | 4 |
| Group IV. . . . . . . . . | 32 | 34 | 32 | 2 |

## Site Comparison

### *Débitage*

The first thing that becomes evident when comparing chippage from the four sites is the different quantities present at each site. Eight times as many artifacts were found at Holcombe as at Paleo-II-W-A but thirty-three times as much chippage was recovered from the Holcombe Site. This suggests some very real functional differences between these sites. It could not be caused by sampling technique since all material was recovered in 1/4-inch hardware cloth and saved from all sites.

I would tend to interpret the gross differences in quantity of débitage as differences in length of occupation. This would also be reflected by the quantity of fire-cracked rock recovered from these sites. The rank ordering for quantity of fire cracked-rock agrees perfectly with the rank ordering for quantity of débitage (Table 44).

In addition to differences in quantities of chippage there are differences in types of flakes and cherts found at these sites. These differences indicate that different types of activity were taking place. Comparisons of flake types are given in Table 45, chert types in Table 46 and average weight of flakes in Table 47.

Holcombe differs radically from the other sites in a high occurrence of block fracture flakes and a high occurrence of dark grey Bayport chert. If the suggested association of these

TABLE 44

CHIPPAGE AND FIRE-CRACKED ROCK

Comparison of Chippage, Total Number of Fire-cracked Rocks and Their Total and Average Weights for the Four Sites Along the Holcombe Beach

| | Holcombe* | Paleo-II | Paleo-II-W | Paleo-II-W-A |
|---|---|---|---|---|
| Total chippage . . . . . | 11078 | 3096 | 1998 | 339 |
| Fire-cracked rock; number. . . . . . . . . | 146 | 30 | 24 | 21 |
| Fire-cracked rock; total weight . . . . . . | 729.9 g | 193.5 g | 74.8 g | 107.2 g |
| Fire-cracked rock; average weight. . . . | 5.4 g | 6.5 g | 3.1 g | 5.1 g |

*UMMA excavation produced 125 fire-cracked rocks with a total weight of 683.1 grams and an average weight of 5.5 grams. The DeVisscher excavations produced 21 fire-cracked rocks with a total weight of 109.8 grams and an average weight of 5.2 grams.

TABLE 45

PERCENTAGE OF FLAKE TYPES

Comparison of the Percentages of Flake Types at the Four Sites

| | Small Retouch Flakes (Per Cent) | Flakes Without Striking Platforms (Per Cent) | Flakes With Striking Platforms (Per Cent) | Block Fracture Flakes (Per Cent) | N |
|---|---|---|---|---|---|
| Holcombe . . . . | 83 | 3 | 2 | 12 | 11078 |
| Paleo-II . . . . . | 92 | 3 | 3 | 2 | 3096 |
| Paleo-II-W . . . | 88 | 4 | 5 | 3 | 1998 |
| Paleo-II-W-A . | 49 | 21 | 22 | 8 | 339 |

two attributes and heat treatment of preforms is valid, this would be one type of activity that would set Holcombe apart from the other sites. It is possible that the longer time period needed to heat, cool, and finish preforms is related to the length of occupation of the site. That is, either preform preparation by heat took place when a group stayed in one place for a longer period of time, or a group remained in one place for several weeks when such preparation was necessary.

TABLE 46

PERCENTAGES OF CHERT TYPES

Comparison of the Percentages of Chert Types at the Four Sites

| | White Bayport (Per Cent) | Light Grey Bayport (Per Cent) | Dark Grey Bayport (Per Cent) | Exotic (Per Cent) | N |
|---|---|---|---|---|---|
| Holcombe . . . . | 25 | 46 | 26 | 3 | 11078 |
| Paleo-II . . . . . | 22 | 63 | 12 | 3 | 3096 |
| Paleo-II-W . . . | 18 | 59 | 9 | 14 | 1998 |
| Paleo-II-W-A . | 37 | 47 | 6 | 10 | 339 |

TABLE 47

AVERAGE WEIGHT OF FLAKES

Average Weight in Grams of the Flake Types from the Four Sites Along the Holcombe Beach

| | Small Retouch Flakes (Grams) | Flakes Without Striking Platforms (Grams) | Flakes With Striking Platforms (Grams) | Block Fracture Flakes (Grams) |
|---|---|---|---|---|
| Holcombe . . . . . | .09 | .72 | .82 | .77 |
| Paleo-II . . . . . . | .10 | .68 | .95 | 1.12 |
| Paleo-II-W . . . . | .10 | .95 | 1.10 | .94 |
| Paleo-II-W-A . . | .13 | .92 | 1.14 | 1.68 |

There are several things which suggest the former condition. Many bone fragments were recovered in the central area of the Holcombe site. In spite of careful screening of the other sites, DeVisscher and Wahla did not find such calcined bones fragments. I would interpret Holcombe as an occupation of several weeks centered around a successful kill while the other sites represent occupations of several days during which time hunting operations met with limited success.

There is also good evidence that preforms were being finished into artifacts at Paleo-II and Paleo-II-W without heat alteration. This is evident in the lower frequencies of block flakes and dark grey chert among the chippage and the relatively constant ratio of points and bases to chippage at all three sites.

If this heat alteration is done to allow greater control while working the artifact, it is reflected in the average weights of flake types from the sites (Table 47). The sites where heat treatment was either not practiced, or practiced to a lesser extent, are marked by larger flakes of all types.

The high percentages of exotic chert at Paleo-II-W should also be noted (Table 46). While this has little meaning when examining the chippage, it will take on significance in our comparison of artifacts from these sites.

Paleo-II-W-A is the most aberrant of these sites not only in quantity of chippage but in type of chippage. An altogether different type of industry seems to be represented at this site. In order to understand this industry we need to know the distribution of *pièce esquille* or possible bipolar cores on the Holcombe beach. One was found at Holcombe, one at Paleo-II, none at Paleo-II-W, and three at Paleo-II-W-A.

I would interpret this distribution in the following manner: Paleo-II-W-A was a small, temporary campsite. It was occupied at a time when few preforms were available. This is the site with both the highest ratios of finished bifaces, to toal artifacts and complete points, to point bases. Little finishing activity took place at this site. The infrequency of preforms is also reflected in the lowest occurrence of dark grey Bayport chert on all three sites. Few preforms were present to heat.

Instead of working with preforms, the knappers used available chert sources—the scattered pebbles in the till of the area. The pebbles were broken on an anvil with the resultant high frequency of bipolar cores. Many of them were unsuitable for further work, hence the relatively low percentage of small retouch flakes and high percentage of inferior white chert, possibly the cortex of local materials. The high percentage of block fracture flakes (Table 45) with an absolutely higher average weight (Table 47) also point to a different chipping technique at Paleo-II-W-A. The occurrence of such a technological variation is striking in light of the uniformity in finished artifacts at all of these sites. Even if the variation occurred in an emergency it does suggest that primitive flint knappers were not so tightly bound by tradition and "motor habits" as some archaeologists have suggested.

## Site Comparisons

### *Artifacts*

As we have mentioned before, the types of artifacts found at these sites are virtually identical. There can be little question that the finished tools were the work of one group of people. There is, however, some variation in frequency of tool types between these sites.

Three classes of artifacts were used to compare the sites: preforms, finished bifaces, and standardized scrapers. Such artifacts as drills and gravers were eliminated from this comparison since so few were found.

The frequencies of these artifact types are given in Table 48. Also included in Table 48 are the ratios of preforms to finished bifaces, preforms to standardized scrapers, preforms to total artifacts used in the analysis, finished bifaces to standardized scrapers, finished bifaces to the total sample and standardized scrapers to the total sample used in the study.

The only uniform ratio is that of finished bifaces to the total sample. On all the sites this class accounts for approximately 50 per cent of the artifacts. In comparison with the total sample Holcombe is marked by a higher percentage of preforms and lower percentage of scrapers. This relative lack of scrapers is also demonstrated in the ratios of preforms to finished bifaces and standardized scrapers. In absolute numbers there are still three times as many standardized scrapers at Holcombe than any of the other sites.

TABLE 48

ARTIFACT CLASSES AND RATIOS

Numbers of Preforms, Finished Bifaces and Standardized Scrapers from the Four Sites and the Ratios of These Classes to Each Other and to the Total

| | Holcombe | Paleo-II | Paleo-II-W | Paleo-II-W-A |
|---|---|---|---|---|
| Preforms . . . . . . | 130 | 7 | . . | 2 |
| Finished bifaces. . | 192 | 27 | 20 | 23 |
| Standardized scrapers. . . . . . | 62 | 21 | 20 | 16 |
| Total . . . . . . | 384 | 55 | 40 | 41 |
| Ratios P/FB . . . . | .68 | .26 | .00 | .09 |
| P/SS . . . . . . . . . | 2.10 | .33 | .00 | .13 |
| P/T. . . . . . . . . . | .34 | .13 | .00 | .05 |
| FB/SS . . . . . . . . | 3.10 | 1.29 | 1.00 | 1.44 |
| FB/T. . . . . . . . . | .50 | .49 | .50 | .56 |
| SS/T . . . . . . . . . | .16 | .38 | .50 | .39 |

Our study of the dèbitage from these sites indicated that heat treatment of preforms was not as common at the smaller sites as it was at Holcombe. The relative lack, or complete absence of preforms at these other sites may be one reason for this. On the other hand, it could be that preforms were hoarded until they could be properly treated.

As DeVisscher and Wahla have previously suggested, the ratio of whole points to point bases varies from site to site. The ratio of points and point bases to total chippage also varies from site to site. These figures are given in Table 49.

TABLE 49

POINTS, BASES AND CHIPPAGE

Numbers of Complete Unreworked Points, Point Bases and Total Chippage From the Four Sites and the Ratios of These Classes to Each Other

| | Holcombe | Paleo-II | Paleo-II-W | Paleo-II-W-A |
|---|---|---|---|---|
| Complete unreworked points . . | 2 | 6 | 1 | 10 |
| Point bases. . . . . | 104 | 13 | 13 | 10 |
| Total chippages . . | 11078 | 3096 | 1998 | 339 |
| Points/bases. . . . | .02 | .46 | .08 | 1.00 |
| Points/chippage. . | .0005 | .0019 | .0005 | .0294 |
| Bases/chippage . . | .0094 | .0042 | .0065 | .0294 |

The Holcombe site and Paleo-II-W are closest in all of these ratios. The interpretation given for the Holcombe site, a place where spears were refurbished, would also hold for Paleo-II-W. This site, however, lacked both preforms and evidence of preform preparation. The high incidence of exotic material among the dèbitage (Table 46) and the occurrence of artifacts of exotic materials mentioned by Wahla and DeVisscher explain this. Fine exotic materials were being finished into projectile points at Paleo-II-W so there was no need for heat treating, a process evidently reserved for poorer quality Bayport chert.

Some refurbishing of spears was done at Paleo-II and Paleo-II-W-A although the low ratios of points to bases (Table 49) suggests that this was not a major activity. The lack of preforms and use of local raw materials is suggested as a cause for these ratios.

## Nature of Site Occupations

The Holcombe site itself appears to have been occupied by several families for a period of several weeks. It is centered around a successful kill of one or more barren-ground caribou. There is evidence from the internal distribution of chippage and artifacts that areas of family occupation, where fires were built for warmth, surrounded a central area where a large fire was used for cooking.

The distribution of chippage indicated that this central area of the site was used for heat treating Bayport chert preforms. In the family areas surrounding the central area there are high concentrations of finished bifaces and small retouch flakes. Several of these family areas may be defined on the basis of distinctive chert profiles in several contiguous units. The primary chipping activities seem to have been directed toward refurbishing spears with new points.

Paleo-II was probably occupied for a shorter period of time. Although no separate provenience was kept on the chippage and there are too few artifacts for a quantitative comparison, the rough distribution map in the original report by DeVisscher and Wahla (1963:56) does suggest some structuring. In the center of the site in an area which they indicate contains fewer than the usual number of small retouch flakes, are a series of "flake knives." These are three of the seven preforms recovered from the site. DeVisscher and Wahla indicate at least three areas of dense artifact concentration surrounding this central area. This might even be further broken down. The settlement pattern would be similar to that of the Holcombe site.

The types of artifacts and chippage recovered from the site indicates that some preforms were being finished to replace broken points. Much of the manufacturing, however, seems to have been directed toward the preparation of scrapers. The ratio of finished bifaces to scrapers is lower at Holcombe than Paleo-II and the ratio of scrapers to total artifacts is twice as high at Paleo-II. Scrapers, as well as projectile points, were the end product of the Paleo-II knappers art. There is a preference for Bayport chert at this site. Perhaps the availability of Bayport chert, coupled with a lack of time for proper preform preparation, caused the high incidence of scrapers and low ratio of points to bases.

Paleo-II-W is also a camp of short duration. There is even less evidence of band structuring here than at the other sites.

The area occupied is considerably less than that at Holcombe. The two possible post molds 13 feet apart are provocative. This is the sole site in the series where absolutely no later artifacts were found. The post molds would have to be associated with the Paleo-Indian occupation. The lack of hearth areas such as we noted at Holcombe is also disturbing.

The chippage and artifacts from the site indicate that projectile points were being made to replace broken ones. It appears that exotic finegrained flints, which needed no application of heat for parallel flaking, were being used instead of Bayport preforms. The average size of fire-cracked rock, which is fairly consistent at the other sites, is considerably smaller at this site. The fact that both DeVisscher and the University of Michigan field party found the same average weight for fire-cracked rock at the Holcombe site suggests that this might have some meaning, perhaps different cooking patterns. The entire picture of Paleo-II-W might suggest a different phase in the seasonal cycle.

Paleo-II-W-A, like the other sites, is unique within the series. The site had been the location of a nineteenth-century dwelling which might have disturbed the pattern of artifact distribution. Although 131 five-foot squares were excavated, an area greater than that excavated at the Holcombe site, only 339 pieces of chippage were found.

The artifact distribution shows some slight indication of clustering but, again, no features or central area were noted. The number of artifacts, however, would indicate an occupation as long as Paleo-II and Paleo-II-W. No features or animal bone were recovered which might indicate success in hunting.

Although the artifacts at the site were identical to those from the other sites the dèbitage seemed to indicate that a different technique for tool manufacturing was employed. A number of possible bipolar cores were recovered, the chert at the site tended to be of a poorer quality, and little final retouch activity took place. In the absence of Bayport preforms, or high quality exotic flint, local pebble sources were utilized. Pebbles from glacial till were broken open and the few good ones were used in tool manufacture. Since most of these would be unsuitable for manufacturing projectile points there is little indication of this type of manufacture.

These four Paleo-Indian sites along the Holcombe beach were obviously occupied by a single culture, perhaps even a single family group. Each of the sites, however, is unique and at each site different types of activity are represented. By a comparison of these sites we have been able to suggest reasons for the variation in artifacts, flake, and chert types along the Holcombe beach ridge.

# IX

## THE LAND OF THE PEOPLE

### The Land

In our initial discussion of the Holcombe beach ridge it became evident that this area was occupied at about 9,000 B. C. for a short period of time. The occupation coincided with the second phase of Lake Algonquin. The association of this material with the second stage of Lake Algonquin is substantiated by the distribution of points similar to those from the Holcombe site in northern Ohio (Prufer, 1964:24) in areas which would have been inundated during the first phase of Lake Algonquin (Hough, 1963: 97).

The sites were located on a sand spit which was only a few feet above the water of Lake Clinton. There is an upward slope to the west but it rises less than 15 feet in the first mile. The streams would have flowed more slowly than today since the stream drop was 25 feet less than the present drop to Lake St. Clair. The entire area was probably marked by small sluggish streams and areas of impounded water.

It is quite likely that the ice front was within several hundred miles of the site. This would mean cold water in the lakes and a generally cooler temperature than today. Paul S. Martin (1958:385) has suggested that this area would be similar to modern treeless tundra or boreal woodland or taiga; the latter was most likely at the time of the Valders maximum. He describes this as "a Savanna formation of needle-leaved trees scattered in a shrub and lichen mat" (1958:379). I would prefer the term "spruce parkland" to described this environmental situation.

In a more recent article Cushing (1965:409-13) has gone into greater detail on the plant cover of the Great Lakes area during this period. He describes a more complex problem of plant succession. Spruce (*Picea*) dominates the earlier horizons and other tree pollen, with the exception of *Populus* (Aspen-poplar), is so rare in many areas that it might be blown in. Herb pollen, particularly wormwood (*Artemisia*), is important.

Cushing emphasizes the difficulty of dealing with the diversity of pollen flora and macroflora. Andersen (1954) suggested that deciduous forest elements in a pollen profile from the Edwin S. George Reserve in Livingstone County, which is not only geographically close to the Holcombe site but dates to the same time period, were redeposited from earlier sediments. With the exception of the deciduous elements he concludes that "the resemblance to the contemporary European vegetation growing under similar conditions near the border of a continental ice sheet is striking. . .Common in both areas are the high frequencies of herb pollen, especially Artemisia, and the occurrence of *Chenopodiaceae, Botrychium, Saxifraga* specimens and, incidentally, also *Polemonium*" (Andersen, 1954:1550).

Cushing feels that Andersen's idea of redeposition cannot be used to explain the occurrence of deciduous forest elements in all situations (1965:410). While viewing the high frequencies of nonarboreal pollen as suggestive of the open vegetation near the northern tree line West (1961) favors the explanation that the deciduous elements are blown in from distant habitats.

In many areas there are suggestions of a primarily herbaceous cover preceding the spruce forest in newly deglaciated areas (Cushing, 1965:412). The emphasis is placed, however, on a diversity of micro habitats". . .as a result of soil instability and fluctuating levels of soil moisture—that could accommodate a diverse flora on the recently deglaciated landscape."

This instability of soils and water levels with the resultant pattern of plant succession is significant for human occupations. Areas recently freed of ice or drained by glacial lakes would have more browse and would, therefore, support larger populations of primary herbivors such as deer, caribou, and mammoth. Areas of mature climax forest might have an equal total biomass but the portion of this available to man would be considerably less. The shores of a shallow lake in a spruce parkland, in the process of draining, would have furnished an optimal environment for the caribou, a primary herbivor which was the prey of the Holcombe hunters.

The swampy conditions suggested by the drainage patterns around the Holcombe site would be ideal for the open spruce parkland conditions described at nearby George Reserve. Under a sparse spruce cover were mugwart, goosefoot, moonwart, saxifrage, and Jacob's-ladder. This would have been the situation at the Holcombe site itself with a greater spruce domination and, perhaps, some deciduous elements further toward the interior of the Michigan lower peninsula.

The sole faunal identification from the Holcombe site is that of barren ground caribou *Rangifer arcticus* (Cleland, 1965). Burt and Grossenheider (1964:234) describe the habitat of these animals as "Tundra in summer, partially open coniferous forest in winter." They observe that after the southward migration in autumn the woodland and barren ground caribou may occur together but their ranges separate after the northward summer migration. Banfield (1961) would group living woodland and barren ground forms into a single species, *Rangifer tarandus*.

Burt and Grossenheider (1964:234) describe the habits of the barren ground caribou in further detail. They always move in large herds, some numering in the tens of thousands; they are migratory and never stay in one place for long. They are excellent swimmers and will often cross a lake rather than go around. While they feed mostly on lichens they also eat herbs, mosses, willows, and grasses; all of which probably existed near the Holcombe site.

Hibbard (1951:235) interpreted the presence of barren ground caribou in Michigan as indicative of tundra conditions. Cleland (1965:350-51) takes a more tempered view and states that ". . . since there is some evidence from pollen diagrams that the floral zones on the fronts of continental glaciers were compressed and probably of mixed composition, the habitat of the barren ground caribou may have been somewhat different from that of modern populations. Nonetheless, it is reasonable to suppose that even in the presence of rapid ecological fluctuation the migrating herd would occupy the cold boreal forest-tundra zone." It is also of interest that all other finds of barren ground caribou in the Michigan lower peninsula are from southeastern Michigan (Halsey, n.d., Hibbard, 1951) within 70 miles of the Holcombe site.

The mammoth and mastodon were present in Michigan at the time of the Holcombe site occupation (Skeels, 1962). Skeels notes (1962:105) that the mastodon ". . .was a forest animal browsing on forest vegetation along bogs and streams" while the mammoth "confined themselves to open grasslands and seldom entered deeply forested areas" (1962:118). The mammoth would be more common in the area of the Holcombe site but mastodon could be found in the not too distant forests. Recent excavations by Wittry (1965) in southeastern Michigan suggest that mastodon, if not actually being hunted, were being used as a food source by man.

In looking at the areas beyond the immediate neighborhood of the Holcombe site we find that the distribution of archaeological materials may help in explaining the occurrence of both closed forest and open spruce parkland plant and animal species in deposits of 9,000 B.C. Where earlier projectile point types (Roosa, 1965) are distributed throughout Michigan (Mason, 1958:4) projectile points similar to those from the Holcombe site are distributed in two north-south corridors; one in eastern Michigan running from Monroe County through eastern Washtenaw to Macomb, Tuscola, and Midland Counties and one in the western part of the state with finds in Berrien, Kent, and Newago Counties.

For now I would offer the following theory. Prior to 9,000 B.C. the entire lower portion of the Michigan lower peninsula might have been open parkland or spruce parkland following the retreat of the ice from the area. An environment such as that described for the Holcombe site was present in large portions of the lower peninsula. By 9,000 B. C. a spruce cover and possibly some pine and even deciduous forest elements were dominant in the central part of the state where present drainage patterns were already established. The distribution of Holcombe points might follow the distribution of open spruce parkland corridors roughly paralleling the Michigan and Huron basins, areas subject to greater soil instability and fluction in water level and drainage patterns.

Butzer (1964:145) has suggested that lower latitude Pleistocene tundras in the Old World, which are roughly equivalent to our spruce parkland, would be among the optimal environments for early hunters. While the comparative biomass available to man for the northern tundra given by Butzer is low, about 800 kilograms of eatable meat per square kilometer, it is also deceptive. It is taken from Banfield's study of contemporary caribou in northern Canada which have been subjected to slaughter with high power rifles, and decimated by fire and competition from the introduction of domesticated reindeer (Burt and Grossenheider, 1964:234). We can automatically postulate a higher biomass by a consideration of the precontact situation and of the animal species other than barren ground caribou that would be present in the area. Butzer (1964:138) also makes a case for a greater biomass on low-latitude tundras over existing tundras. "There can be no doubt that these Pleistocene low-latitude tundras had a tremendous carrying capacity, somethwat greater than the recent, higher-latitude tundras." Differences in drainage patterns and extended periods of hibernal darkness in higher latitudes are cited as reasons for this conclusion. These same factors would affect the carrying capacity of low-latitude spruce parkland.

The land of the Holcombe people was far from a hostile environment. It might have been similar to Butzer's (1964:138) forest-tundra in the Old World: "The ecological environment of the forest-tundra is optimal in as much as cold environments are concerned. The migratory gregarious herds of the open country seek winter refuge here where many species, faced with a deep snow cover, can augment their diets by consumption of tree shoots and bark. Arboreal groves provide windbreaks during storms, while the immediate environment provides all that the tundra otherwise offers. For the human occupant, an added hunting element of forest species is provided." This, perhaps, provides a brief description of the land of the Holcombe people.

## The People

Among many primitive hunters only members of the group are considered fully human. They think of themselves as "the Men" or "the People." The people who lived along the Holcombe beach, no doubt, considered themselves to be "the People." It is now five years since I first set foot on the Holcombe beach and during this time I have also come to think of them as the People.

The subsistance pattern of the People furnishes us with a theoretical problem. Some archaeologists seem to be certain that Paleo-Indian hunters were solely big game hunters. Other archaeologists have felt that the term "foraging" (Ritchie, 1956:73) might be more realistic. Griffin has observed that ". . .faunal elements that were probably contemporary with muskox, mastodon and mammoth in the Late Glacial include the barren-ground caribou, giant beaver, peccary, giant moose, and probably other species now in the boreal forest or tundra. Certainly this smaller game would have been numerically more abundant and easier for the early hunters to kill" (1965:658). Griffin has concluded (1964:224) that, "the restriction of the diet of these early hunters to 'big game' animals has been by certain archaeologists, not the people of 10,000 to 8,000 B.C."

The food resources available to the Barren-Ground Eskimos today have been described by Mowat (1952:106) for an environment that was certainly less productive than suggested for the Holcombe beach: "Well, the Barrens are not given to the deer alone. In the winter, great numbers of arctic hares move down from the northern fringes of the Barrens, and they make delicious and tender food. Then there are the ptarmigan, whose numbers are so great in the spring and fall that the flocks may cover the hills like snow. The rivers and lakes are literally filled with white fish, trout, grayling and suckers and these can be netted in quantity during the summer." "The Ihalmiut travel light, and a man of the People crossing the open plains in the summer carries little more than a knife, a pipe and perhaps a spare pair of skin boots called *kamik*. He eats when he finds something to eat. There are usually suckers in the shrunken streams, and these can sometimes be caught with the hands. Or if suckers are too hard to find, the traveler can take a length of rawhide line and snare the orange-colored ground squirrels on the sandy esker slopes. In early summer there are always eggs, or flightless birds, and if the eggs are nearly at the hatching point, so much the better" (Mowat, 1952:83).

Going a bit further afield, MacNeish (1964:532) has suggested that the earliest inhabitants of the valley of Tehuacan might be best described as plant and animal collectors. In another article I suggested that the many and diverse local lithic industries in the eastern United States were a reflection of adaptations to local resources and hunting conditions (Fitting, 1965*a*).

The faunal remains from the Holcombe site and the late glacial environment of the four sites would indicate that meat in general, and the barren ground caribou in particular, played a large role in the diets and lives of the People.

Mowat (1952:101) described the preferred diet of the Barren-Ground Eskimo with vivid detail. "The cooking varied somewhat but the food did not. The rule was meat at every meal and nothing else but meat, unless you could count a few well-rotted duck eggs which served as apetizers. To satisfy my curiosity I tried to estimate the quantity of meat Hekwaw put away each day. I discovered that he could handle ten to fifteen pounds when he was really hungry—though otherwise he probably subsisted on somewhat less." The words for "food" and "deer," meaning caribou, were practically synonymous.

In an earlier article I drew on Services' (1962:59-190) description of the band level of development for a model of the expected patterns of Paleo-Indian social organization and settlement pattern (Fitting, 1965*a*). The Holcombe site fitted the model with indications of five to eight males and a total population of twenty to fifty individuals. At the Holcombe site these were arranged around a central area. Rough flint-working was done in the central area while finishing of distinct chert types, was done in the family areas. I postulated that preforms were held communally in the center of the camp. Arnold Pilling has since described a similar situation among the Twi of Bathurst and Melville Islands. Here individual males will travel great distances to obtain supplies of valued raw material. When they return to the camp this is placed in a central area. Other males come to this area and ceremonially beg the owners to share the raw material with them. This process is known as "bludging" and it accomplishes a distribution of raw material to all members of the group. At the same time individuals are allowed to acquire prestige for getting, and later sharing, this raw material.

An integral part of band organization is the existence of band territories. While it is possible to talk theoretically about free wandering (Beardsley, and others, 1956) it has never been observed as the pattern of living groups. While the first inhabitants of this area might, in theory, have been free wanderers, the People were later occupants (Griffin, 1965; Roosa, 1965) and would be classed as restricted wanderers (Beardsley, and others, 1956:136).

We observed that the Holcombe beach was characterized by an open spruce parkland environment such as that where the barren-ground caribou winter today. If the Holcombe beach was located toward the southern part of the range of the caribou, it would also be located toward the southern part of the range of the People. We observed that 97 per cent of the lithic material from the Holcombe site was Bayport chert. This chert is found in the Upper Grand Rapids limestone formations located 100 miles to the north of the Holcombe beach.

An example of a projectile point similar to those from the Holcombe beach was found near Cat Lake in Tuscola County and donated to the Museum of Anthropology by E. W. Hyde. During the summer of 1965, William B. Roosa and Henry Wright observed another such point from eastern Midland County in the collection of Eldon Cornelius. These finds, both of Bayport chert, indicate that the people traveled to the north.

Similar points have also been reported in a north-south corridor along the western part of the state. George Davis of Grand Rapids has two projectile point bases from a site near Aetna in northern Newago County. Both are of Bayport chert which is not as common in the western part of the state as it is in the eastern part. Another similar point of a dark grey Bayport was found in Kent County by Buerl Guernsey of Gowen, Michigan on the Steffenson site south of Bass Lake. Guernsey also found a Holcombe point of an exotic material on the Hoxie farm near Wabsis Lake in Kent County. Amos Green of Eau Claire has pointed out two similar points from Berrien County from the

Franz site. Neither was of Bayport chert. The occurrence of Bayport chert in the northern part of this corridor may have more significance when the distribution patterns and possible band territories in this area are better understood.

In eastern Michigan it is possible to be more specific about band territories. Artifacts similar to those from the Holcombe site have been found in northern Ohio (Prufer, 1964; Prufer and Sofsky, 1965). They have a distribution suggesting a range along the south shore of Lake Erie. Prufer and Sofsky's (1965) recent report on the McKibben site in Trumbul County offers an excellent comparison for the Holcombe beach. At the McKibben site there is a Holcombe-like component. The chert at McKibben, however, is primarily from local sources. The nine specimens illustrated in the report are "all made of black or slate-blue Upper Mercer flint" (Prufer and Sofsky, 1965:13). In a group of artifacts which Prufer sent to Arthur J. Jelinek at the University of Michigan Museum of Anthropology for examination, I also observed a projectile point base made of Bayport chert. At the Holcombe site a single point base and 2 per cent of the chippage were Upper Mercer flint derived from Ohio sources.

At first examination it would appear that the distribution of typical Holcombe artifact forms would represent the range of the People. This would mean a total range of at least 400 miles, perhaps more if we take the western Michigan material into consideration.

This situation would have precedent among the Barren-Ground Eskimo. After describing the settlement pattern of the band Mowat states that ". . .thus, within a radius of three miles of each other, dwelt all of the living People in a land which stretches for five-hundred miles from south to north, and three-hundred miles from east to west" (1952:92).

Here the situation of the Holcombe People differs drastically from that of the Deer People. The environment of the Holcombe people was, as we have suggested, much richer and the population density was probably higher. The basic settlement pattern indicates the effect of this population density. Mowat's People were forced to live miles apart "for there is not enough willow scrub to support the cooking fires of more than three families at any single spot" (1952:92). Where the Deer People faced 500 miles of low-carrying capacity tundra, the Holcombe People looked to a narrow corridor of high-carrying capacity, low latitude spruce parkland. The eleven scattered families of the Deer People could have clustered around a single fire in the richer land of the Holcombe People.

The interpretation I would favor for the artifact distribution which we have observed would be that of similar peoples occupying contiguous territories. The artifacts of these groups would be similar with a preference for local raw materials. These groups would be in contact with each other and marriage and trade probably took place between them. This would account for the slight overlap of raw materials in both the Michigan and Ohio sites.

At the Holcombe site there is one area where a knapper had a supply of Ohio chert. At Paleo-II-W it was perhaps Upper Mercer flint that was "bludged" rather than Bayport preforms. The young men seeking honor and prestige for acquiring raw material perhaps made a habit of traveling in different directions from year to year. The as yet undefined cherts from western Michigan may represent still another band group which wandered in the western spruce parkland corridor at the same time.

With such groups we would more than halve the suggested band territories to less than 200 miles. This does not seem unreasonable in light of the carrying capacity of the land. In fact, further research might reduce the size of the territories and increase the number of bands. Arnold Pilling, who has lived with band groups, feels that even 150 miles is too great a range. Again, this is a subject for further investigation.

With the People located within a territory we can look at their seasonal cycle. The Holcombe beach is located to the south of the flint sources and in the southern part of the range of the barren ground caribou. While this may not be the ultimate winter camp of the People, it is, no doubt, a point somewhere near the southern phase of their seasonal movement. Mowat's description, again, seems very close to what the life of the Holcombe People must have been like (1952:132-36):

> The spring was a time of great killing and yet the People took only enough in those days to meet their needs until fall. For the hides of the spring deer are useless for clothing and the meat is lean and lacking in fat.
>
> There was much gorging on fresh meat in the spring, for when the sun again stands high in the sky, the bellies of men revolt from the dry meat and frozen meat that is their diet all winter.
>
> After the herds had passed by to the north, the People moved their camps up the slopes of the hills so that the long winds could battle the flies which were coming. Here the People lived until mid-summer, awaiting the return of the deer.
>
> Summer was the time of eggs and young birds. Even the children went daily out over the plains with their toy slings and bows to search

for the eggs and the young of the ptarmigan, of the curlew, the ducks and even the tiny song birds of the Barrens. The men too did not let their hunting skills grow rusty, for they searched out the dens of the great arctic wolves and took enough pelts for mats and the triming of parkas.

By midsummer the first herds of does were again passing down into the land of the People, and for a month the hunting was done out on the plains. At this time of the year, and until the deer again swing to the north, the skins were still of little value, except for those of the fawns, and there was no need for a large kill. So the hunters went out with the bows made of the springy horn of the muskox, and they stalked the deer over the hills and killed only a few, picking the fatest beasts with great care.

At last, in late summer, the herds again swung to the north and passed out of the Ihalmiut land. This was the time of greatest activity during the year, for it was known that when the deer came back again it would be only for a brief few days as they fled south before the approach of winter.

The last rotten ice was all gone from the rivers and from most of the lakes before fall so the deer followed new routes, swinging along the curved shores of the great lakes and crossing rivers just below or above open bodies of water. . . .To these places the People now moved their tents. . . .In the old days the Ihalmiut told me about, there would be thirty or forty tents near each of the seven most famous crossings, and there would be many scores of tents at other minor crossings scattered over the land.

Then on a day in October there would be snow in the air. A kayak would sweep up the river out of the north and the man in it held his spear aloft as a signal. "They come!" was the cry. . . .This was the time of great slaughter.

In the camps huge fires burned all day and night and blocks of white deer fat began to mount up in the tents. On the bushes which spread their dead leaves in the hollows, thin slices of meat were laid out to dry until the valleys and hills about the camp by the crossing glowed a dull red under the waning sun.

Then it was winter and the great herds were gone but there still remained game to hunt out on the bleak winter plains.

And even more in the forest-tundra land of the Holcombe people.

This is how it must have been for the few years, certainly not more than a few generations, that the People lived in the land. Lake Clinton vanished rapidly with the fall of Lake Algonquin. The low stage in the Great Lakes, over 400 feet lower than the Algonquin high in the Huron Basin, was reached in less than 1,500 years (Hough, 1963:103). The land, as the People knew it, lasted only a few centuries at most.

The drop of water level, the warmer temperatures which followed the retreat of the ice, the new forest cover, first a full, closed cover of spruce, later pine and some broad-leaved trees, meant a new way of life. Gone were the herds, the familiar animals and birds. The optimal open spruce parkland was replaced by the marginal closed boreal forest. The People must have fled, spread, and changed their ways in order to survive. They either changed to a way of life far different from that which we have suggested, or died out entirely; this we will never know. All we can deal with is a brief moment in the lives of the People.

# X

## EARLY MAN IN THE NEW WORLD: A VIEW FROM THE SHORES OF LAKE CLINTON

### Some Considerations

Several decades ago Walter Taylor decried the overwhelming emphasis on the comparative, or taxonomic, approach in American archaeology. He wrote (1948:95) that "the apparent be-all and end-all of archaeological excavation appears to be the placing of the resultant finds in one or another of the taxonomic pigeonholes, and a glance at the *Conclusions* of most monographs will show them to be chiefly concerned with comparative studies and seldom with the cultural integration or implication of the data themselves."

My study of the Holcombe People ended with Chapter IX, this section is a bow to the format of contemporary archaeological literature. It was the most difficult part of this monograph to write. On a cold, clear day the opposite shore of Lake Clinton stands sharply in view; as one looks thousands of miles into the distance, or years into the past or future, the vision becomes first opaque, then darkened. For the past five years my primary research interest, if not activity, has been the study of early man in Michigan. While learning how much I did not know about this subject, my confidence in the extant interpretations of the Paleo-Indian occupation of the New World diminished proportionately. It is with a feeling bordering on sheer terror that I leave the familiar confines of the southwest shore of Lake Clinton.

One problem in comparative studies is the nature of much of the data with which one must make comparisons. There is a near mystical isolation of a field of "Paleo-Indian Studies." While most American archaeologists have been developing an anthropological approach to the interpretation of their subject matter, "Paleo-Indianists" have become, if anything, more historically and typologically oriented.

There has been a widespread tendency to view the terms

"Paleo Indian" and "fluted point" as being one and the same. I am not in any way opposed to typological and distributional studies. They are very useful, almost essential, because of the sparse data with which they deal. Such studies are not, however, studies of Paleo-Indian culture. I applaud honest titles to studies of points like Roosa's (1965) "Some Great Lakes Fluted Point Types" and the Cleveland Museum series, *Survey of Ohio Fluted Points*, prepared by Prufer and his associates (Prufer, 1960*a*, 1960 *b*, 1961, 1962*a*, 1962*b*, 1963*b*, 1964; Prufer and Chinn, 1960, Prufer and Munro, 1961*a*, 1961*b*).

The above instances of projectile point typology are examples of the better projectile point studies. I am in agreement with most of their "conclusions" (used in the comparative sense again). There are, of course, many examples of projectile point interpretations carried to almost absurd extremes. One prominent archaeologist who examined the Holcombe site collection noted a formal resemblance to the points from the Scharbauer site as described by Wendorf and others (1955) and insisted that since they fitted Wormington's (1957:262-63) definition of Midland Points a cultural continuity existed between Texas and southeastern Michigan. "After all," he observed, "they were a free wandering people."

This line of reasoning leads to a search for "genetic" relationships of projectile points. In spite of Brew's (1946:58) arguments against this type of classification it still appears in the literature:

> A hypothetical double shouldered Sandia I point, with an ovate body and contracting stem, would resemble the Hell Gap point in both style and flaking technique. It is possible that the relation of Sandia I to the Plano tradition is identical to that of Sandia II to the fluted tradition. The two types of Sandia points may be forerunners of these two traditions or they may be local hybrids having affinities with the clovis fluted point and the Hell Gap Plano point (Agogino and Rovner, 1964:240).

There is an inherent danger in naming point types. By giving objects names it is possible to compare names with little regard to the actual artifacts, let alone their possible cultural significance. Calling the points from the sites along the Holcombe beach Midland Points would be a classic example of acultural typing of artifacts. Calling them Holcombe Points, which I have tried to avoid, might facilitate the writing of this report but would probably lead to future confusion. I have a feeling that if we were to define a Holcombe Point today, we could expect to wake up tomorrow and find someone in Oklahoma or Alabama "mendelizing" its ancestry out of Angostura by Merserve.

It is not the descriptive categories that I dislike, it is the substitution of name comparisons for artifact comparisons to which I would object. To state, as Haynes (1964:1408) does, that ". . .variations within individual collections are as great as variations between collections. . . ." is to avoid the problems of attribute clustering, local traditions, and even individual style, by ignoring them. Roosa's (1965) detailed descriptions of fluting and finishing techniques are to be preferred to Haynes' catchall Clovis category. Roosa, on the other hand has ignored metric variation as an indication of function and clines of size distribution and has rationalized this by citing the existence of size variation among his otherwise carefully defined point types. To be consistent in my criticism, I have ignored fluting patterns in studies of metric variation (Fitting, 1965*b*, 1965*c*) and have begged the question in the same manner by citing variation in local areas and collections with no detailed study for possible clustering.

We have now come the full circle from a criticism of the isolating report to the realization that we are guilty of the very thing to which we have objected. With this recognition of fallibility we can indulge further in a series of the "it-looks-like-a-thus-and-so" summaries so common to American archaeology.

## Early Man in the New World

There has been a strong movement in the past few years for the recognition of extremely ancient industries in the new world (Krieger, 1962, 1964). I find these arguments, based on a massive accumulation of tenuous evidence, to be unacceptable. Following the arguments advanced by Jelinek (1965*a*) I would relegate man's entry into the New World to a post 14,000 B.C. time period, perhaps even later. I would also follow Haynes (1964) and Mason (1962) in placing the fluted point complexes at the base of the cultural column in the area east of the Rocky Mountains (including their reservations on Sandia).

There are industries which are probably older than that from the Holcombe beach even in Michigan (Peru, 1965; Roosa, 1965) but I am also becoming convinced of an extremely close clustering of early man site dates. Haynes (1964:1408) has an average age of 11,260 ± 360 years for a group of six Clovis samples. The Holcombe site has been geochronologically dated to a period just prior to 11,000 years ago and the Debert site in Nova Scotia, if placed at the Valders times (Beyers, 1965), is roughly contemporary. This does not invalidate the suggested sequence of Paleo-Indian culture change; it might, however, compress previous time estimates. Griffin (1965:660) feels that ". . .the best interpretation of the age of the fluted points in the northeast is that they are primarily older than 9,000 B.C." Haynes (1964:1410) feels that the Llano complex, his earliest fluted point complex, could not be earlier than 12,000 years ago.

If the pattern of point distribution suggested earlier for Michigan holds true, the apparently earlier point forms in Michigan are older by a few centuries rather than a few millenia. Their distribution in the state reflects the distribution of open parkland and open spruce parkland areas existing prior to the Valder's maximum in the same way that the distribution of the point forms similar to those from the Holcombe beach reflects the distribution of the open spruce parkland at that time.

As we have mentioned, the Holcombe People were pursuing a way of life which could not exist in the area of Lake Clinton for long after 9,000 B.C. They have been characterized as "the last gasp of the Paleo-hunters in this area." I would continue to view them as falling into Mason's (1962:233) Late Paleo-Indian subdivision. Griffin has preferred to call this site Early Archaic (1965:660) and views it as being the beginning of a series of regional adaptations that are increasingly emphasized throughout the Archaic period. Mason (1962:234-35) has emphasized the diversity of early projectile point forms in eastern North America. I have interpreted this diversity (Fitting, 1965*a*), along with the clines of metric diversity, as being indicative of adaptions to local conditions. The regional adaptations characteristic of the Archaic, as Griffin views it, would then be present prior to the time of occupation of the Holcombe beach ridge. Not having a fixed point for the origin of regional adaptations I would fall back to Mason's typological criterion which emphasizes a formal continuity that Griffin (1965:660) admits has some validity.

## Site Comparisons

There are a few other Paleo-Indian sites in the Grea Lakes area which furnish us with some comparative material. The Barnes site near Midland would furnish one such area for comparison but only some of the projectile point descriptions have been published (Roosa, 1963, 1965). In going over slides from the site I have noted the presence of preforms similar to those from

Holcombe, only larger, and both end scrapers and convergent tip scrapers. From both Roosa's descriptions and my own observations I would say that the projectile point forms are very different. This is also true for Roosa's Lux site material and for the artifacts from the Dobbelaar site described by Peru (1965).

In western Michigan the Hi-Lo site (Fitting, 1963*b*) has produced cultural material with a Paleo-Indian cast to it which is distributed all over the southern parts of the lower peninsula (Fitting, 1963*a*). The projectile point forms are larger and cruder than those from the Holcombe site. End scrapers similar to those from Holcombe were found at the Hi-Lo site but other tool types were lacking. Considering the very limited collection from the site this is not too surprising.

The Brohm site on the north shore of Lake Superior (MacNeish, 1952) is another very interesting site within the area. The illustrated projectile points show similarities to those from the Holcombe beach ridge. The basal thinning is not as pronounced and the points are all larger than those from Holcombe. This, however, could be a result of the material used to manufacture them. Preforms are present although the quarry area is only a short distance away (they are called ovoid blades by MacNeish). Large chopping tools, like we found in slate at Holcombe, are present at Brohm in taconite and quartzite. The end scrapers from the two sites are similar and several of the minor tool types from Holcombe might also be present. There is one possible blade tool (called a strike-a-light) and one object reminiscent of our convergent tip scrapers (called a possible basal fragment of a crude contracting stemmed point).

In 1952 MacNeish dated this site to some time after the Lake Algonquin maximum. Hough (1963:97) has demonstrated that this area was covered by ice during the Algonquin high stage. Quimby (1959:424) has related this site to one of a series of post Algonquin beaches which would mean that it was occupied after the Holcombe beach ridge had been abandoned and Lake Clinton had vanished. The Brohm assemblage is the kind of assemblage one might expect to be made on the north shore of Lake Superior by the cultural descendants of the Holcombe People who were following the open forest-tundra to the north with the retreat of the ice although it may also have come in from the prairies.

Mason (1963) has recognized similar Late Paleo-Indian points from collections in Wisconsin. He also has reported a number of stemmed forms similar to those from the Rennier site (Mason and Irwin, 1960), and to forms found on Manitoulin Island and in parts of

Ohio (Prufer, 1963*a*; Prufer and Baby, 1963:31-43). I think that there would be little dispute that the stemmed point forms are representative of complexes which post date the Holcombe site and are typologically dissimilar. We shall not pursue their significance beyond recalling DeVisscher and Wahla's observation that these forms, as well as Hi-Lo points, are found within the bed of Lake Clinton.

We have already noted the occurrence of projectile points like those from Holcombe in Northern Ohio (Prufer, 1964; Prufer and Sofsky, 1965). The distribution of these points is within the bed of the first phase of Lake Algonquin but in an area unaffected by the second phase which was not present in the Erie basin, and which helped us to date the actual occupation of the Holcombe beach ridge. This is an area where we might hope to find an occupation similar to that on the Holcombe beach. The several publications already cited by Prufer and his associates suggest an intensive Paleo-Indian occupation for most of Ohio.

In going beyond the upper Great Lakes area I shall confine myself to observations on a few of the better documented sites in the Northeast—Reagen, Bull Brook, Williamson, and Shoop.

In reading Ritchie's (1953) report on the Reagen site in Vermont one is struck with many similarities to the Holcombe beach situation. While Ritchie originally suggested a date of some time prior to 4,000 B.C. for the site more recent interpretations by Mason (1960) and Griffin (1965:659) would make this occupation roughly contemporary with the occupation of the Holcombe beach.

The Reagen site collection was obtained from an exposed area of approximately two acres. Ritchie noted that it was a camp of some size but suggested that it represented repeated occupation rather than the presence of a single large group.

The occurrence of exotic raw material intrigued Ritchie and he suggested that some was imported from areas as much as 100 miles away. He noted the presence of some small amount of black flint.

The ratio of chips to artifacts is disturbing—179 artifacts are mentioned, and only 68 chips. The author did state that many stone flakes and chips still litter the sand, so perhaps no systematic attempt was made to collect this material.

Ritchie's two end scraper categories are represented at the Holcombe beach and his side scrapers could be broken down into several tool types described from Holcombe, primarily convergent tip scrapers and concave scrapers on blades. His combined gravers and scrapers are familiar as are this retouched or utilized flake tools. There is nothing equivalent to the Reagen shouldered knives at the Holcombe site. From the illustrations and descriptions I would interpret his lanceolate knives as preforms.

The projectile points and point bases vary from those found along the Holcombe beach. Both collections, however, vary from unfluted to fully fluted forms and are marked by their diminutive, even delicate, manufacture. I would view Reagen as representing the same kind of local adaptation to changing environmental conditions that we found around Lake Clinton.

The Bull Brook site near Ipswich, Massachusetts, is another site which we must examine (Beyers, 1954, 1955, 1956). There is a radio-carbon date for this site of 7,000 B. C. (Beyers, 1959). Mason (1962:238) and Griffin (1965:658) have both rejected this date; the former on typological grounds and the latter because of the lack of clear association with cultural material (the same thing that occurred with the radiocarbon sample from the Holcombe site). Beyers, on the other hand, has objected to ". . .assigning the Bull Brook site an age greater than that permitted by the radiocarbon dates without a considerable body of substantial evidence" (1962:247).

There is little similarity between the projectile points from the two localities. There is, however, a duplication of scraper, graver, and even drill types. Douglas Jordan (personal communication) has described an object from the site which sounds like the *pièce esquille,* or possible bipolar core fragments which we recovered from the Holcombe area. I also have the impression that preforms are rare; so perhaps a different types of lithic industry is present.

I am not sure how the "hot spots" from the site should be interpreted. They are suggestive of a series of family occupation areas similar to those from the Holcombe site itself. They are, however, at greater distances and some are apparently as productive as some of the smaller loci along the Holcombe beach. It is very possible that they represent repeated, short-term, band occupations.

Beyers' (1955) description of features sounds like a description of the Holcombe site features. I am also interested in this recovery of long bone fragments which might have been deer. They also might have been caribou. In any event, the adaptation, if not the technology, is very similar to that found in the Lake Clinton area.

The Williamson site in Dinwiddie County, Virginia (McCary,

1952) is as far away from the upper lakes as I shall stray for comparative material. The over-all picture is similar; the projectile point forms are different but the types of the other tools are similar, including perforators, end scrapers, and convergent-tip scrapers. McCary noted that the cherts selected at this site were foreign to the area. He noted a lack of chippage and cores but mentioned "16 fluted basal ends of knives" which I would class as preforms. Here too, exotic material is being carried to the site from some distance in the shape of preforms.

I would also suspect, from McCary's description, that the mile length of the site is not a continuous occupation; that it could be broken down into a series of local occupations like those along the Holcombe beach ridge.

The most detailed and comprehensive of the eastern Paleo-Indian reports is Witthoft's (1952) discussion of the Shoop site in Pennsylvania. His description of the site (1952:467-68) is so striking as to bear repeating:

> If the Site itself were any thinner it would not be a site. Eleven very slightly elevated areas on the flat hilltop, often more than a hundred yards apart, and generally less than thirty feet in diameter, usually yield about a half-dozen chips of all sorts and one or two artifacts after each cultivation. Areas between these productive spots are probably not barren because of erosion, else we would find industrial material on the slopes below. This spotty distribution of material seems to represent the original nature of the site, and probably each spot represents a different camp or separate hearth within a camp.

On the basis of the Holcombe situation I would favor the former interpretation.

Witthoft also makes a point of the importation of preforms of Onondaga chert from quaries in western New York. The occurrence of finegrained black chert as a minority types is also of interest since similar material was found at Holcombe, McKibben, and Reagen. One point and two retouch flakes of this material were found at Shoop and Witthoft, while not certain of the source, suggested a Lehigh County origin.

I am just as surprised as Witthoft at the low ratio of chips to artifacts. The closest we come to this ratio is at Paleo-II-W-A where there are less than seven chips per artifact. Several factors might affect this. Along the Holcombe beach the sites with the higher ratios of scrapers to finished bifaces showed less evidence of manufacturing activity than the Holcombe site itself. The highest ratio of standardized scrapers to total artifacts was at Paleo-II-W and this was .50. For the Gordon collection from the Shoop site this ratio is .79. If a high percentage of scrapers signifies a concern with activities other than finishing projectile points then this might be the explanation for the low ratio of chips to artifacts at Shoop.

Witthoft also found evidences of heat alteration (1952:473-74):

> About ten percent of the chips and tools show evidence of fire. Four of the jasper artifacts are burned red, by the roasting of their coloring limonite. A higher proportion of chips than tools show fire spalling but but this distinctive type of non-conchoidal shattering out of surface is conspicuous on all types of tools. I cannot remember handling any series from any other site with so high a proportion of fire spalled chips.

He did note the presence of "block spalls of chert, triangular or prismatic in cross-section tapered and of no regular form. . . ." but associated these with "hammer broken blocks. . .the result of gross breakage and coarse trimming." Since the artifacts from the site are manufactured from preforms there would be no place for such coarse trimming and I would tend to view these as low-temperature heat fractures.

Most of the tool forms described for Shoop are present along the Holcombe beach. The "used-up remnants of polyhedral or cylindrical flint cores" are similar to what we have called *pièce esquille*, or possible bipolar core fragments. Along the Holcombe beach these objects occurred in the greatest number at the site with the lowest ratio of chips to artifacts. End scrapers, concave scrapers on blades, convergent tip scrapers, denticulate scrapers, gravers, and combination tools are present in both areas.

The preforms from Shoop are of interest because of their close similarity to the preforms from the Holcombe beach. Witthoft did not note the presence of edge grinding as a part of preform preparation but he did mention that grinding was found on finished points.

The finishing and fluting technique used on the points are vastly different from those found at Holcombe. Personally, I would give more weight to the similarities of settlement pattern and over-all technology than to the discontinuity of a single class of artifacts.

Three other sites should be mentioned because of the prominence which they shall have in the literature over the next few years. Only brief notes have appeared on the Debert site (Stuckenrath, 1964) in Nova Scotia and the Well's Creek site in Tennesse (Dragoo, 1965) and Olaf Prufer's excavation of the Welling site in Ohio during the summer of 1965.

Dragoo has a site at Well's Creek with quantities of large artifacts. Dragoo has seen the series of tools from Holcombe and feels that they are similar to those from Well's Creek with the consideration of the limited size of the Holcombe chert sources.

The artifacts from Welling are also more massive but sources for chert are located near by. One thing which I noted from the Welling site was the occurrence of large preforms with ground edges. I saw several flakes of bifacial retouch with ground edges and Prufer said that there were more. I would speculate that the same type of manufacture of artifacts from preforms was practiced at this site.

The Debert site, a chronological contemporary of the Holcombe beach occupation, is perhaps the most important of all of these sites. The industry seems to reflect the same type of adaptation to local conditions. Douglas Beyers, after reading an early draft of the Holcombe report, wrote, "As I read over your report on the Holcombe site, I have thought from time to time that I was reading a description of the Debert site." The same type of artifact clustering, feature concentrations and flake types are present. Beyers noted the presence of *pièce esquille* and suggested (1965) that some of the Debert artifacts were treated with heat to facilitate flaking.

## The Holcombe Beach

Returning from our tour of northeastern North America the Holcombe beach ridge occupation still stands unique. It does, however, show certain similarities with a wide range of sites throughout this area which can be placed in approximately the same time period. It is one of a myriad of local traditions. These local traditions can furnish us with a basis for studying the local adaptations, ranges, movements and patterns of exchange that have only been hinted at in the reported material from the northeast.

## REFERENCES


Agogino, George, and Irwin Rovener
1964 Paleo-Indian Traditions: A Current Evaluation. Archaeology, Vol. 17, No. 4, pp. 237-43. New York.

Anderson, Svend Th.
1954 A Lake-Glacial Pollen Diagram from Southern Michigan, U.S.A. Danmarks Geologiske Undersøgelse, Vol. 2, No. 80, pp. 140-55. København, Denmark.

Banfield, Alexander W. F.
1961 A Revision of the Reindeer and Caribou Genus *Rangifer*. National Museum of Canada Bulletin, No. 177. Ottawa.

Bay, James W.
1938 Glacial History of Streams of Southeastern Michigan. Cranbrook Institute of Science Bulletin, No. 12. Bloomfield Hills.

Beardsley, Richard K., Preston Holder, Alex D. Drieger, Betty J. Megers, John B. Rinaldo, Paul Kutsche
1956 Functional Implications of Community Patterning. Memoirs of the Society for American Archaeology, No. 11, pp. 129-57. Salt Lake City.

Byers, Douglas
1954 Bullbrook - A Fluted Point Site in Ipswich, Massachusetts. *American Antiquity*, Vol. 19, No. 4, pp. 343-51. Salt Lake City.
1955 Additional Information on the Bullbrook Site, Massachusetts. *Ibid.*, Vol. 20, No. 3, pp. 274-76, Salt Lake City.
1956 Ipswich, B. C. Essex Institute Historical Collections. Essex, Massachusetts.
1959 Radiocarbon Dates for the Bullbook Site. American Antiquity, Vol. 24, No. 4, pp. 427-29. Salt Lake City.
1962 Comment on "The Paleo-Indian Tradition in Eastern North America" by Ronald J. Mason. Current Anthropology, Vol. 3, No. 3, pp. 247-50. Chicago.
1965 The Debert Archaeological Project: A Brief Statement. Paper Presented at the 30th Annual Meeting of the Society For American Archaeology. Urbana, Ill.

Brew, J. O.
1946 Archaeology of Alkalai Ridge, Southeastern Utah. Papers of the Peabody Museum of American Archaeology and Ethnology, Vol. 21. Cambridge.

Broecker, W. S., and Farrand, W. R.
1963 Radiocarbon Age Of The Two Creeks Forest Bed. Geological Society of America Bulletin, Vol. 74, pp. 795-802.

Burt, William H., and Richard P. Grossenheider
1964 A Field Guide to Mammals. Boston: Houghton Mifflin Company.

Butzer, Karl W.
1964 Environment and Archaeology. Chicago: Aldine Publishing Company.

Cleland, Charles E.
1965 Barren Ground Caribou *Rangifer arcticus* From an Early Man Site in Southeastern Michigan. American Antiquity, Vol. 30, No. 3, pp. 350-51. Salt Lake City.

Cushing, Edward J.
1965 Problems In The Quarternary Phytogeography of the Great Lakes Region. *In:* The Quarternary of the United States, edited by H. E. Wright Jr. and David G. Frey. Princeton, N.J.: Princeton University Press.

DeVisscher, Jerry, and Edward J. Wahla
1963 The DeVisscher Paleo II Occupation Site. The Totem Pole, Vol. 46, No. 6, pp. 44-57. Detroit.
1964*a* Paleo-II-W: A Minor Paleo-Indian Occupation Site In Macomb County Michigan. Michigan Archaeologist, Vol. 10, No. 1, pp. 5-10. Ann Arbor.
1964*b* Paleo-II-W, A Minor Paleo Occupation Site in Macomb County, Michigan. The Totem Pole, Vol. 47, No. 8, 10 unnumbered pages. Detroit.

Dice, Lee R.
1943 The Biotic Provinces of North America. Ann Arbor: The University of Michigan Press.

Dragoo, Don
1965 Investigations At A Paleo-Indian Site in Stewart County, Tennessee. Eastern States Archaeological Federation Bulletin, No. 24, pp. 12-13. Philadelphia.

Dustin, Fred
1935 A Study of The Bayport Chert. Papers of the Michigan Academy of Science, Arts, and Letters, Vol. 20 (1934 meeting), pp. 465-75. Ann Arbor.

Epstein, Jeremiah F.
1960 Burins From Texas. American Antiquity, Vol. 26, No. 1, pp. 93-7. Salt Lake City.
1963 The Burin-Faceted Projectile Point. *Ibid.*, Vol. 29, No. 2, pp. 187-201. Salt Lake City.

Fitting, James E.
1963*a* An Early Post Fluted Point Tradition in Michigan: A Distributional Analysis. Michigan Archaeologist, Vol. 9, No. 2, pp. 21-24. Ann Arbor.
1963*b* The Hi-Lo Site: A Late Paleo-Indian Site in Western Michigan. The Wisconsin Archeologist, Vol. 44, No. 2, pp. 87-96. Lake Mills.

Fitting, James E.

1964*a* Bifurcate-Stemmed Projectile Points in the Eastern United States. American Antiquity, Vol. 30, No. 1, pp. 92-4. Salt Lake City.

1964*b* Some Characteristics of Projectile Point Bases From The Holcombe Site, Macomb County, Michigan. Papers of The Michigan Academy of Science, Arts, and Letters, Vol. 49 (1963 meeting), pp. 231-39. Ann Arbor.

1965*a* Observations on Paleo-Indian Adaptive and Settlement Patterns. The Michigan Archaeologist, Vol. 11, Nos. 3-4, pp. 103-9. Ann Arbor.

1965*b* A Preliminary Report on a Quantitative Examination of Paleo-Indian Projectile Points in the Eastern United States. Papers of The Michigan Academy of Science, Arts, and Letters, Vol. 50 (1964 meeting), pp. 365-71. Ann Arbor.

1965*c* A Quantitative Examination of Virginia Fluted Points. American Antiquity, Vol. 30, No. 4, pp. 484-91. Salt Lake City.

Griffin, James B.

1964 The Northeastern Woodland Area. *In*: Prehistoric Man In The New World, ed. Jesse D. Jennings and Edward Norbeck. Chicago: The University of Chicago Press.

1964 Late Quarternary Prehistory in The Northeastern Woodlands. *In*: The Quarternary of The United States, ed. by H. E. Wright, Jr., and David G. Frey. Princeton, N. J.: Princeton University Press.

Handley, C. O., Jr.

1953 Marine Mammals in Michigan Pleistocene Beaches. Journal of Mammology, Vol. 34, No. 2, pp. 250-56.

Halsey, John R.

n.d. The Distribution of Some Pleistocene Mammals in the Eastern United States. The Michigan Archaeologist. In press.

Haynes, C. Vance, Jr.

1964 Fluted Projectile Points: Their Age and Dispersion. Science, Vol. 145, No. 3639, pp. 1408-13. Washington, D. C.

Hibbard, Claude W.

1951 Remains of Barren Ground Caribou in Pleistocene Deposits of Michigan. Papers of The Michigan Academy of Science, Arts, and Letters, Vol. 37, pp. 235-37. Ann Arbor.

Hough, Jack L.

1958 Geology of The Great Lakes. Urbana: University of Illinois Press.

1963 The Prehistoric Great Lakes of North America. The American Scientist, Vol. 51, No. 1, pp. 84-109. Princeton, N.J.

Jelinek, Arthur J.

1962 The Use Of The Cumulative Graph in Temporal Ordering. American Antiquity, Vol. 28, No. 2, pp. 241-43. Salt Lake City.

Jelinek, Arthur J.
1965*a* Man's Role in the Extinction of Pleistocene Faunas. Paper presented at the INQUA Symposium on Pleistocene Extinction. Boulder, Colo.
1965*b* The Upper Paleolithic Revolution and the Peoplings of the New World. The Michigan Archaeologist, Vol. 11, Nos. 3-4, pp. 85-88. Ann Arbor.

Keslin, Richard O.
1964 The Holcombe Site, Macomb County, Michigan. Paper presented at the 1964 meeting of the Michigan Academy of Science, Arts, and Letters. Ann Arbor.

Krieger, Alex D.
1962 The Earliest Cultures in the Western United States. American Antiquity, Vol. 28, No. 2, pp. 138-43. Salt Lake City.
1964 Early Man in the New World. *In*: Prehistoric Man in the New World, ed. Jesse D. Jennings, and Edward Norbeck. Chicago: The University of Chicago Press.

Leverett, Frank, and Frank B. Taylor
1915 The Pleistocene of Michigan and Indiana and the History of the Great Lakes. U. S. Geological Survey Monograph 53. Washington, D. C.

MacNeish, Richard S.
1952 A Possible Early Site in Ontario. National Museum of Canada, Bulletin No. 126, pp. 23-47. Ottawa.
1964 Ancient Mesoamerican Civilization. Science, Vol. 143, No. 3606, pp. 531. Washington, D. C.

McCary, Ben C.
1951 A Workshop Site of Early Man in Dinwiddie County, Virginia. American Antiquity, Vol. 17, No. 1, pp. 9-17. Salt Lake City.

Martin, Paul S.
1958 Pleistocene Ecology and Biogeography of North American. *In*: Zoogeography, ed. C. L. Hubbs. American Association for the Advancement of Science.

Mason, Ronald J.
1958 Late Pleistocene Geochronology and the Paleo-Indian Penetration of the Lower Michigan Peninsula. Anthropological Papers, Museum of Anthropology, University of Michigan, No. 11. Ann Arbor.
1960 Early Man and the Age of the Champlain Sea. The Journal of Geology, Vol. 68, pp. 366-76. Chicago: The University of Chicago Press.
1962 The Paleo-Indian Tradition in Eastern North America. Current Anthropology, Vol. 3, No. 3, pp. 227-78. Chicago.
1963 Two Late Paleo-Indian Complexes in Wisconsin. The Wisconsin Archeologist, Vol. 44, No. 4, pp. 199-211. Lake Mills.

Mason, Ronald J., and Carol Irwin
1960 An Eden-Scottsbluff Burial in Northeastern Wisconsin. American Antiquity, Vol. 26, No. 1, pp. 43-57. Salt Lake City.

Mowat, Farley
1952 People of the Deer. Boston: Little, Brown and Company.

Peru, Don
1965 The Distribution of Fluted Points in the Counties of Kent and Allegan, Michigan. The Michigan Archaeologist, Vol. 11, No. 1, pp. 1-8. Ann Arbor.

Peske, G. Richard
1963 Argillite of Michigan: A Preliminary Projectile Point Classification and Temporal Placement from Surface Materials. Papers of the Michigan Academy of Science, Arts, and Letters, Vol. 48, pp. 557-66. Ann Arbor.

Prufer, Olaf H.
1960*a* Survey of Ohio Fluted Points, No. 1, Cleveland Museum of Natural History, Cleveland.
1960*b* *Ibid.*, No. 3.
1961 *Ibid.*, No. 4.
1962*a* *Ibid.*, No. 7.
1962*b* *Ibid.*, No. 8.
1963*a* The McConnell Site: A Late Paleo-Indian Workshop in Coshocton Co., Ohio. Scientific Publications of the Cleveland Museum of Natural History, n.s. Vol. 2, No. 1. Cleveland.
1963*b* Survey of Ohio Fluted Points, No. 9. Cleveland Museum of Natural History. Cleveland.
1964 *Ibid.*, No. 10.

Prufer, Olaf H., and Raymond S. Baby
1963 Palaeo-Indians of Ohio. The Ohio State Historical Society. Columbus.

Prufer, Olaf H., and Garretson W. Chinn
1960 Survey of Ohio Fluted Points, No. 2. Cleveland Museum of Natural History. Cleveland.

Prufer, Olaf H., and Elisabeth C. Munro
1961*a* Survey of Ohio Fluted Points, No. 5. *Ibid.*
1961*b* *Ibid.*, No. 6.

Prufer, Olaf H., and Charles Sosky
1965 The McKibben Site (33 TR-57), Trumbull County, Ohio: A Contribution to the Late Paleo-Indian and Archaic Phases of Ohio. The Michigan Archaeologist, Vol. 11, No. 1, pp. 9-40, Ann Arbor.

Quimby, George I.
1959 Lanceolate Points and Fossil Beaches in the Upper Great Lakes Region. American Antiquity, Vol. 24, No. 4, pp. 424-26. Salt Lake City.

1960 Indian Life in the Upper Great Lakes. Chicago: The University of Chicago Press.

Ritchie, William A.
1953 A Probable Paleo-Indian Site in Vermont. American Antiquity, Vol. 18, No. 3, pp. 249-58. Salt Lake City.

Ritchie, William A.
1956 Prehistoric Settlement Patterns in North Eastern North America. *In*: Prehistoric Settlement Patterns in the New World, ed. Gordon R. Willey. Viking Fund Publications in Anthropology, No. 23. New York.

Roosa, William B.
1963 Some Michigan Fluted Point Sites and Types. The Michigan Archaeologist, Vol. 9, No. 3, pp. 44-48. Ann Arbor.
1965 Some Great Lakes Fluted Point Types and Sites. *Ibid.*, Vol. 11, Nos. 3-4, pp. 89-102. Ann Arbor.

Service, Elman R.
1962 Primitive Social Organization: An Evolutionary Perspective. New York: Random House.

Skeels, Margaret Anne
1962 The Mastodons and Mammoths of Michigan. Papers of the Michigan Academy of Science, Arts, and Letters, Vol. 47 (1961 meeting), pp. 101-33. Ann Arbor.

Spaulding, Albert C.
1960 Statistical Description and Comparison of Artifact Assemblages. *In*: The Application of Quantitative Methods in Archaeology, ed. Robert F. Heizer and Sherborne F. Cook. Viking Fund Publications in Anthropology, No. 28, pp. 60-83. Chicago.

Stuckenrath, Robert, Jr.
1964 The Debert Site: Early Man in the Northeast. Expedition, Vol. 7, No. 1, pp. 20-29. Pittsburgh.

Taylor, Walter W.
1948 A Study of Archaeology. American Anthropological Association Memoir No. 69. Menasha, Wis.

Wendorf, Fred, Alex A. Krieger, Claude C. Albritton, T. D. Stewart
1955 The Midland Discovery. University of Texas Press. Austin, Texas.

West, R. G.
1961 Late - and - Post Glacial Vegetational History in Wisconsin, Particularly Changes Associated with the Valders Readvance. American Journal of Science, Vol. 259, pp. 766-83.

White, Anta M.
1963 Analytic Description of the Chipped-stone Industry from Snyders Site, Calhoun County, Illinois. Museum of Anthropology, The University of Michigan, Anthropological Paper No. 19, pp. 1-70. Ann Arbor.

Witthoft, John
1952 A Paleo-Indian Site in Eastern Pennsylvania: An Early Hunting Culture. Proceedings of the American Philosophical Society, Vol. 96, No. 4, pp. 464-95. Philadelphia.

Wittry, Warren L.
1965 The Institute Digs a Mastodon. Cranbrook Institute of

Science Newsletter, Vol. 35, No. 2, pp. 14-18. Bloomfield Hills, Mich.

Wormington, H. M.
1957 Ancient Man in North America. Denver Museum of Natural History Popular Series, No. 4. Denver.

Yarnell, Richard Asa
1964 Aboriginal Relationships Between Culture and Plant Life in the Upper Great Lakes Region. Museum of Anthropology, University of Michigan Anthropological Paper No. 23. Ann Arbor.

PLATE I

Fig. 1

Fig. 2

The Holcombe site. Fig. 1. Looking east along the Holcombe Beach ridge. Fig. 2. Feature Number 2 with block fracture flakes and bone fragments in place.

PLATE II

Flake Types from the Holcombe site.
*a*, Block fracture flakes; *b*, flakes of bifacial retouch with striking platforms (see Figure 4); *c*, small retouch flakes.

PLATE III

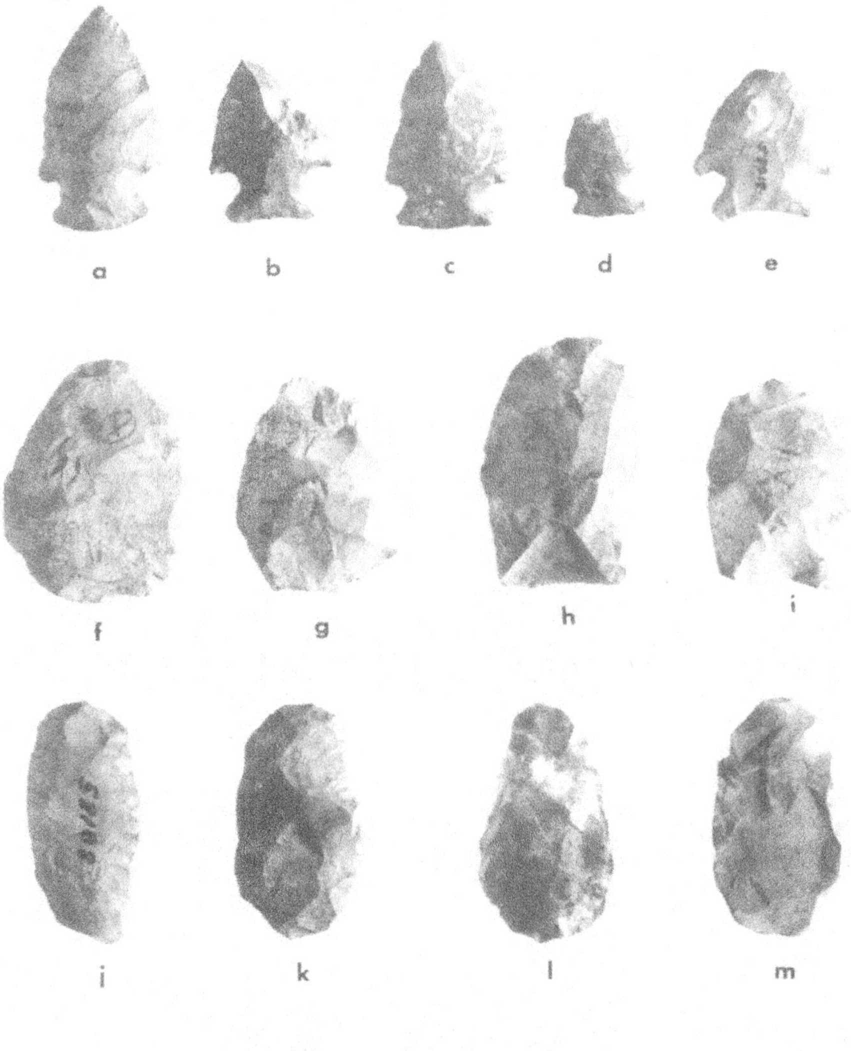


Artifacts from the Holcombe site.
*a-e*, side notched points; *f-i*, Type A preforms, *j-m*, Type B preforms.

PLATE IV

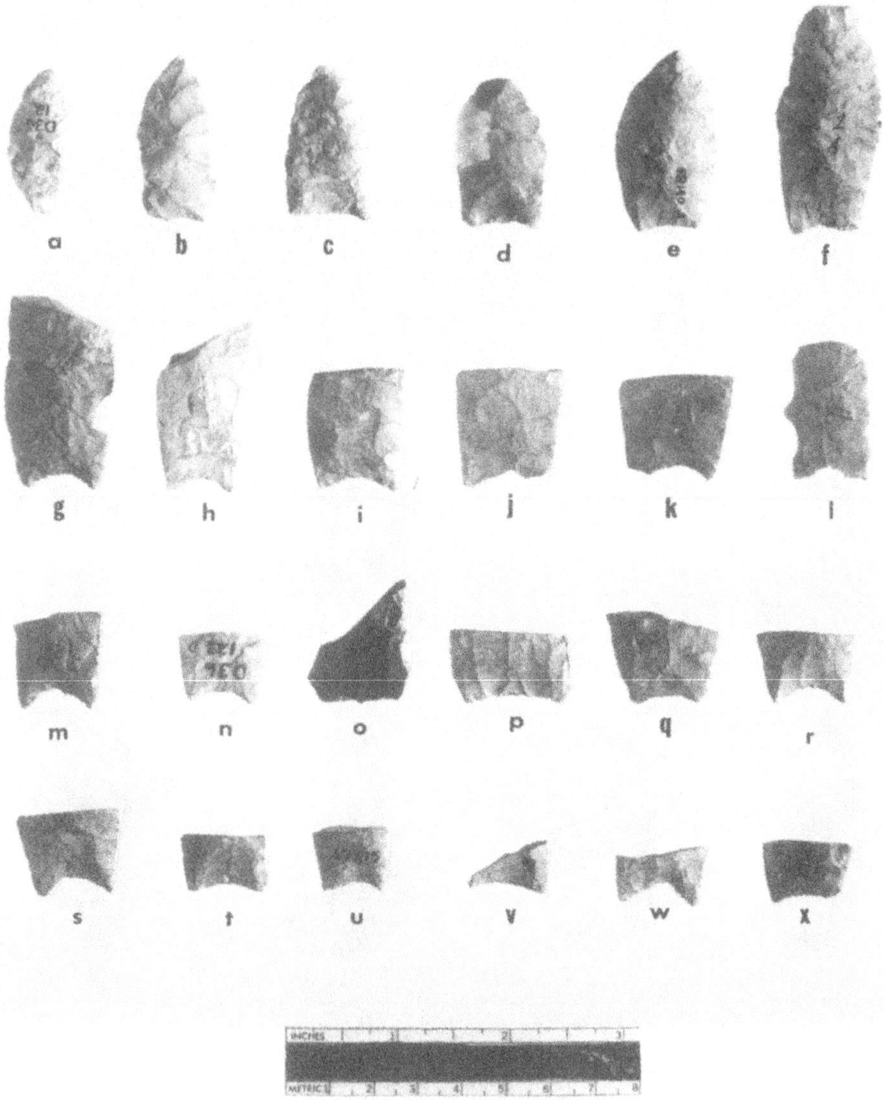


Artifacts from the Holcombe site.
*a-f*, projectile points, *g-h*, projectile point bases.

PLATE V

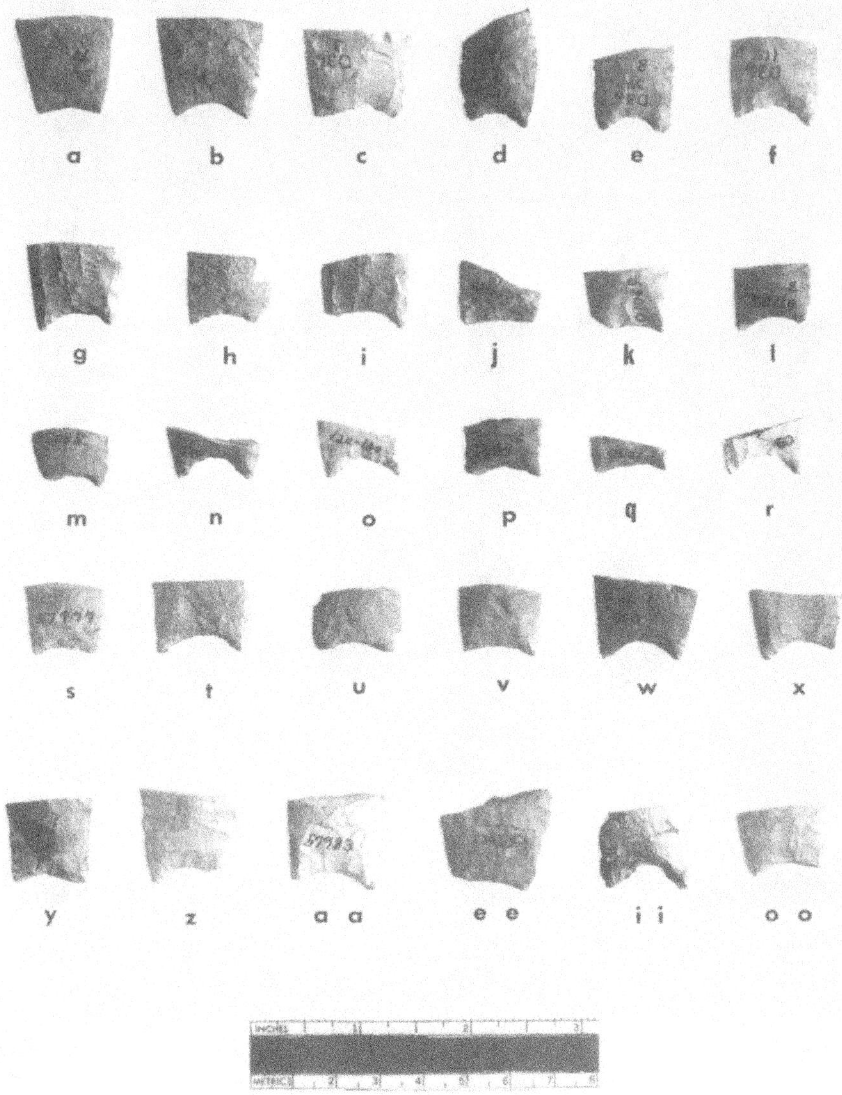

Artifacts from the Holcombe site.
*a-oo*, projectile point bases.

PLATE VI

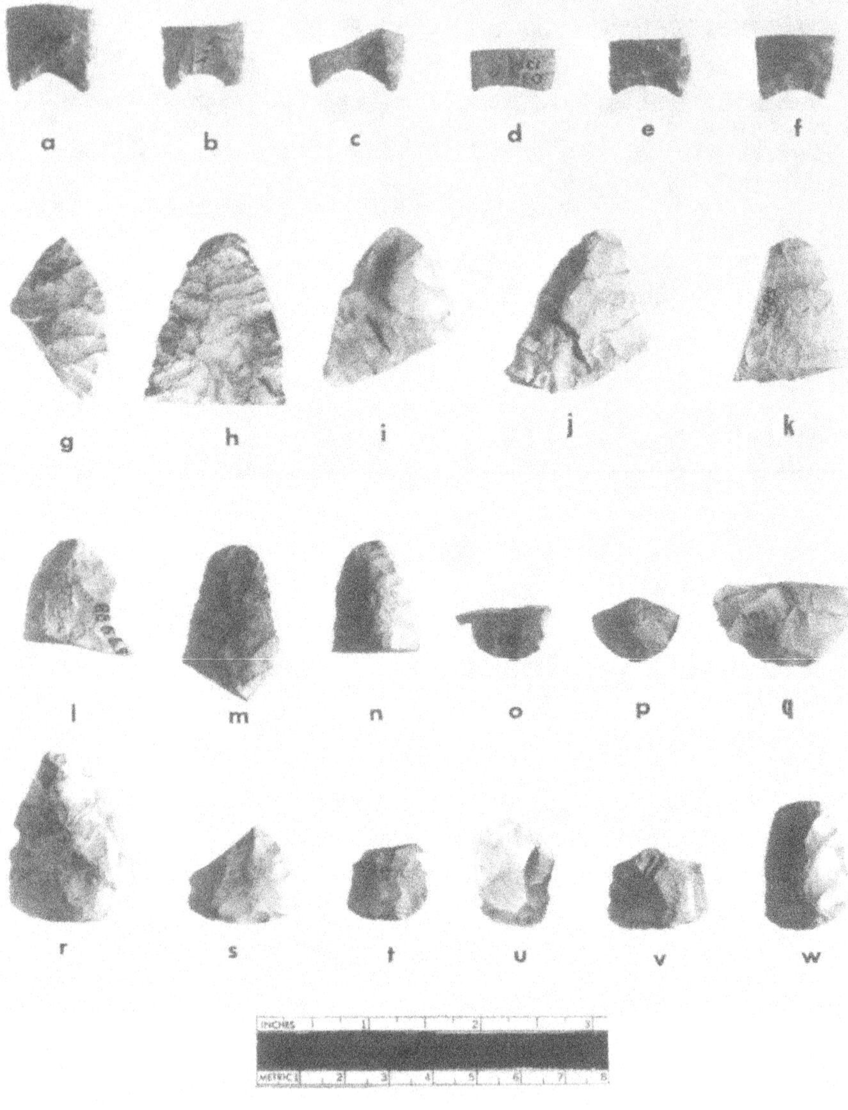


Artifacts from the Holcombe site.
*a-f*, projectile point bases; *g*, pointed tip; *h-n*, convergent tips; *o-q*, rounded tips; *r-w*, end scrapers.

PLATE VII

Bifacially worked slate object from the Holcombe site.

PLATE VIII

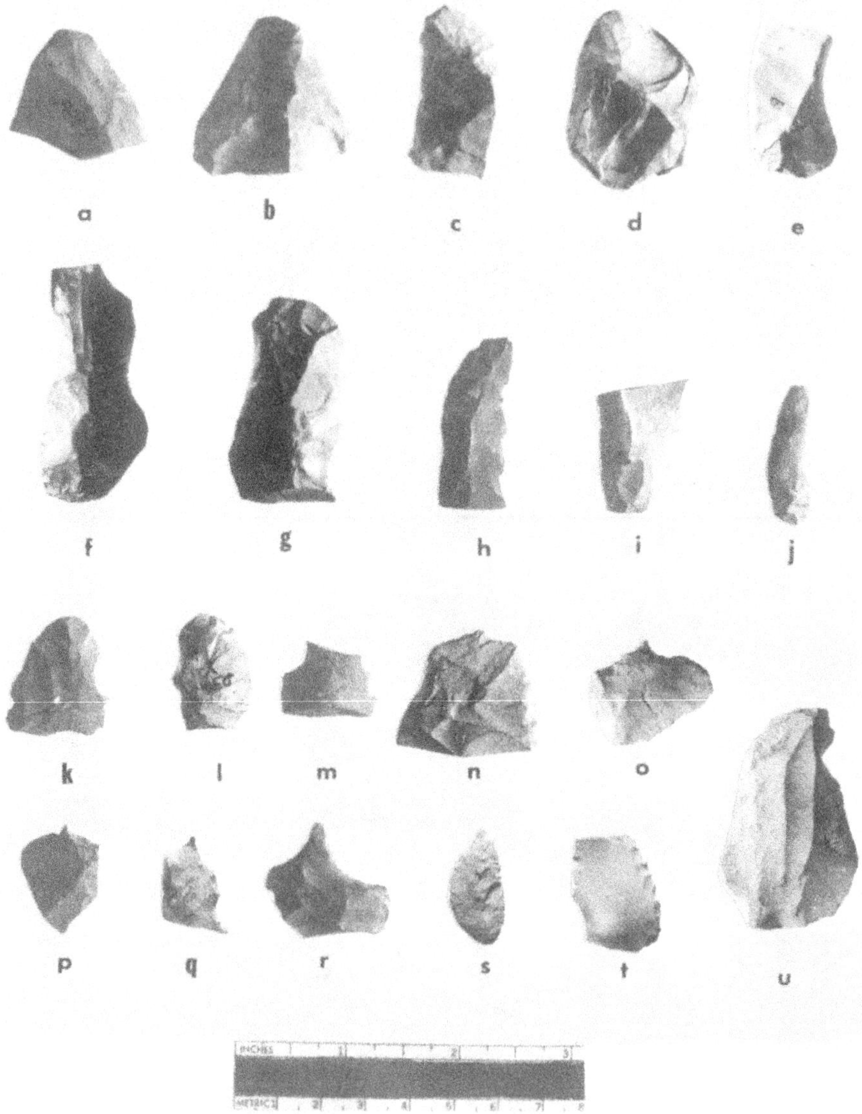


Artifacts from the Holcombe site. *a-d*, steep retouch convergent tip scrapers; *e-g*, concave scrapers on blades; *h-i*, retouched blades; *j*, unretouched blade; *k*, concave scraper on a flake; *l-m*, concave scrapers on bifaces; *n-q*, gravers; *r*, drill fragments; *s*, crescent-shaped flake with a blunted back; *t*, flake with retouch on bulbar surface; *u*, LeVallois flake.

PLATE IX

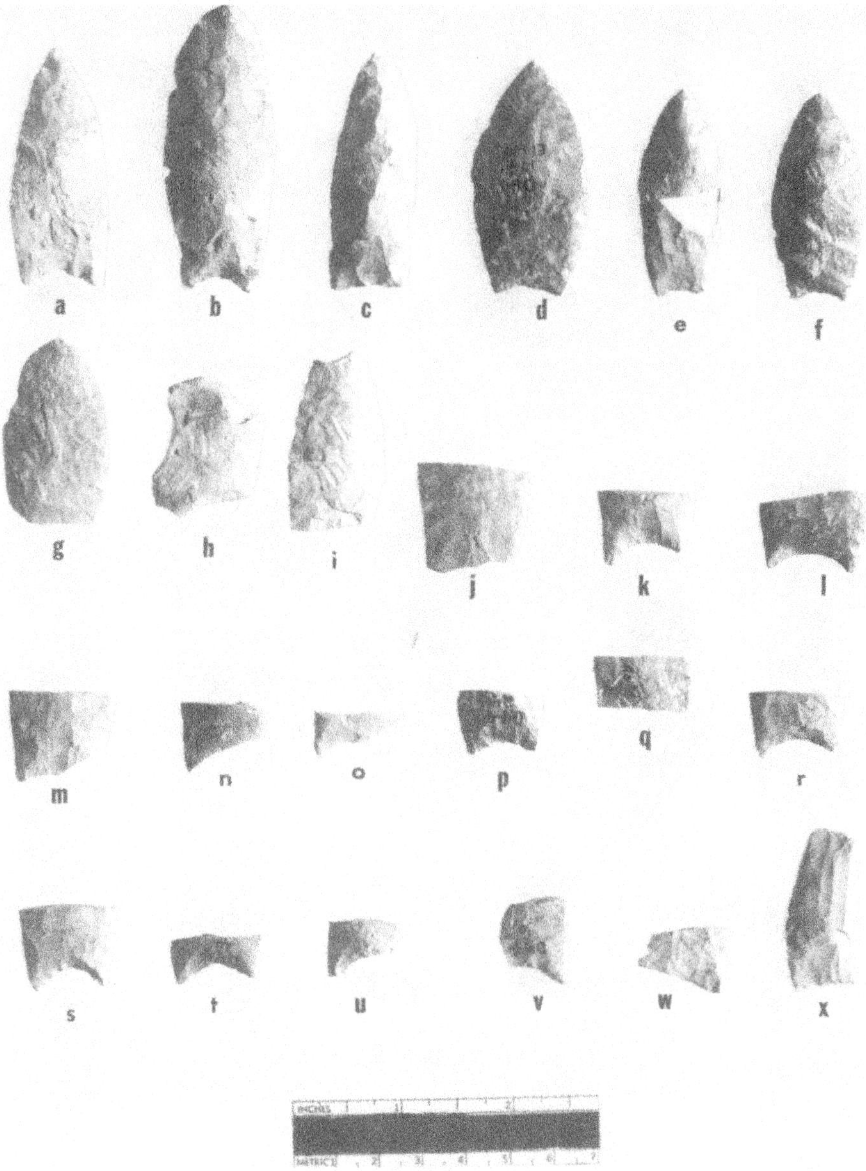


Artifacts from Paleo-II. Projectile points and point fragments.

PLATE X

Artifacts from Paleo-II. *a-d*, preforms; *f-g*, medial fragments; *h*, spokeshave scraper; *i-k*, scrapers; *l*, Fragment of a spokeshave scraper; *m-v*, scrapers; *w*, drill.

PLATE XI

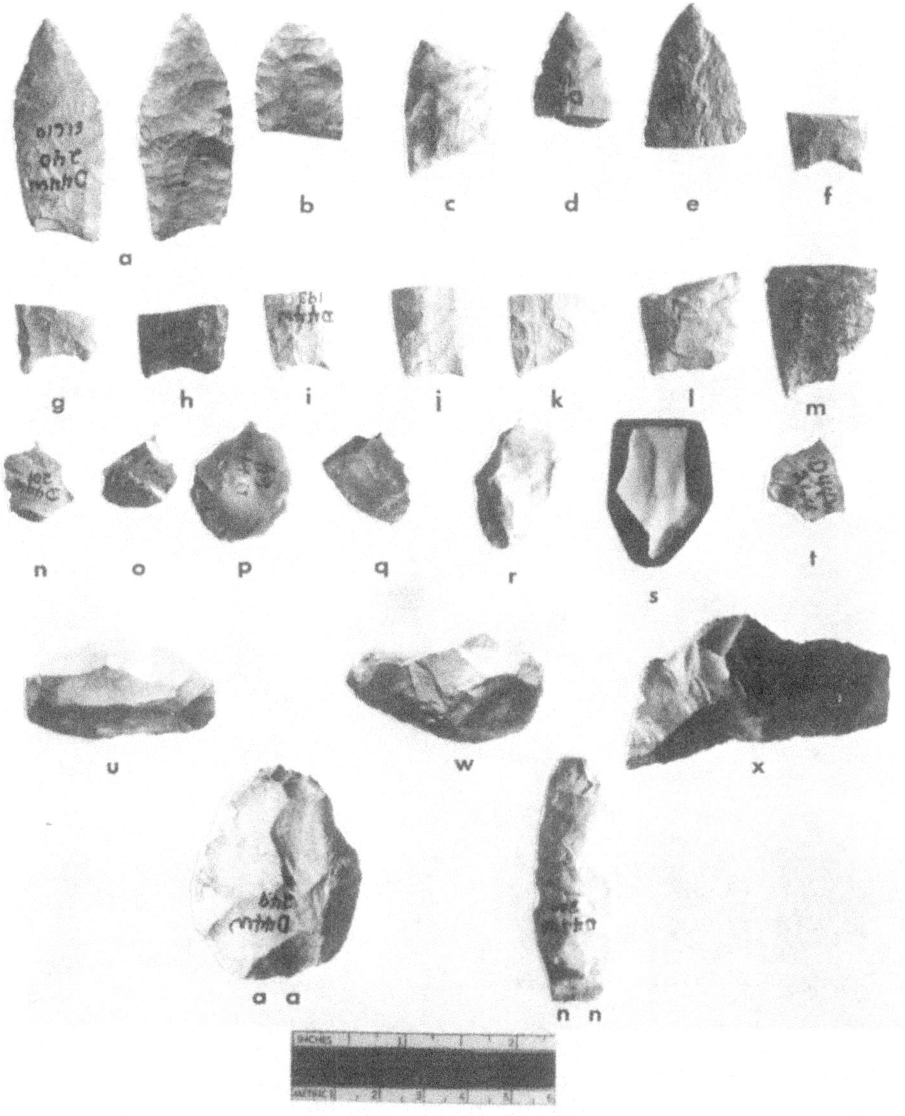


Artifacts from Paleo-II-W. *a*, projectile points; *b-e*, point tips and fragments; *f-m*, point bases; *n-t*, gravers; *u-x*, scrapers; *x*, *aa*, preform; *nn*, convergent biface.

PLATE XII

Artifacts from Paleo-II-W-A. *a-g*, points and point fragments; *h-n*, point bases; *o*, convergent biface tip; *p-v*, scrapers; *w-y*, gravers; *z*, *ee*, utilized flakes.

E-0266-155-13c

www.ingramcontent.com/pod-product-compliance
Lightning Source LLC
LaVergne TN
LVHW050021250826
846302LV00008B/53
*9781949098181*